From Your Head To Your Heart:

The Change You Long For Is Just 18 Inches Away

MARIA DURSO

Unless otherwise noted, all Scripture quotations are from the Holy Bible, New International Version®, NIV®. Copyright © 1973, 1978, 1984, 2011 by Biblica, Inc.™ Used by permission of Zondervan. All rights reserved worldwide. www.zondervan.com. The "NIV" and "New International Version" are trademarks registered in the United States Patent and Trademark Office by Biblica, Inc.™

Scripture quotations marked asv are from the American Standard Bible.

Scripture quotations marked esv are from the Holy Bible, English Standard Version. Copyright © 2001 by Crossway Bibles, a division of Good News Publishers. Used by permission.

Scripture quotations marked kjv are from the King James Version of the Bible.

Scripture quotations marked mev are from the Holy Bible, Modern English Version. Copyright © 2014 by Military Bible Association. Used by permission. All rights reserved.

Scripture quotations marked nas are from the New American Standard Bible, copyright © 1960, 1962, 1963, 1968, 1971, 1972, 1973, 1975, 1977, 1995 by The Lockman Foundation. Used by permission. (www.Lockman.org)

Scripture quotations marked ncv are from The Holy Bible, New Century Version. Copyright © 1987, 1988, 1991 by Word Publishing, Dallas, Texas 75039. Used by permission.

Scripture quotations marked nkjv are from the New King James Version®. Copyright © 1982 by Thomas Nelson. Used by permission. All rights reserved.

Scripture quotations marked nlt are from the Holy Bible, New Living Translation, copyright © 1996, 2004, 2007. Used by permission of Tyndale House Publishers, Inc., Wheaton, IL 60189. All rights reserved.

Scripture quotations marked The Message are from *The Message: The Bible in Contemporary English*, copyright © 1993, 1994, 1995, 1996, 2000, 2001, 2002. Used by permission of NavPress Publishing Group.

Scripture quotations marked tlb are from The Living Bible. Copyright © 1971. Used by permission of Tyndale House Publishers, Inc., Wheaton, IL 60189. All rights reserved.

Book Cover Design by Fabian Alvarez
ISBN: 1507791178
ISBN-13: 978-1507791172

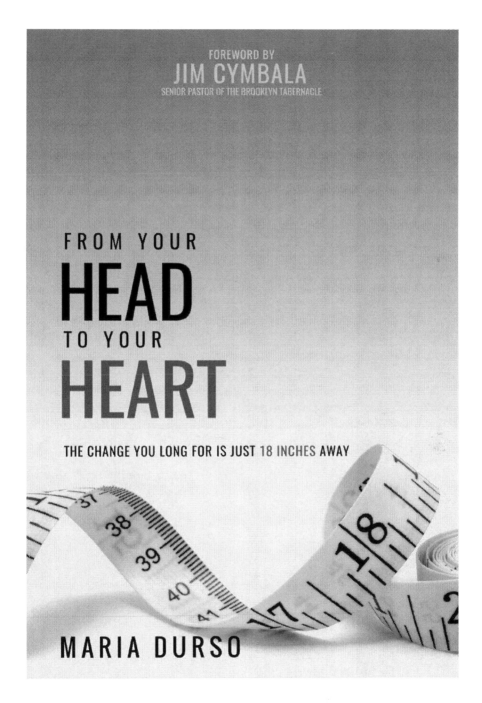

FOREWORD BY
JIM CYMBALA
SENIOR PASTOR OF THE BROOKLYN TABERNACLE

FROM YOUR
HEAD
TO YOUR
HEART

THE CHANGE YOU LONG FOR IS JUST 18 INCHES AWAY

MARIA DURSO

Wow! Maria has hit the target in this much-needed book. She knows intimately the difference between the head and the heart. Our culture's tendency to try to figure out life and its challenges intellectually is facing a battle that, without this revelation from Scripture, cannot be won. You and I have to realize that our feelings will betray us at every step. We can't analyze God's forgiveness and love for us. The key is our heart. The apostle Paul tells us in Ephesians 1 that we have been blessed with every spiritual blessing. But it's hard to realize the vastness of this truth. We need to have His spirit of wisdom and revelation to fully grasp His love and have our hearts mended and healed. Only then can we walk by faith and not by sight or by feeling.

Michael and Maria Durso are both living and walking miracles. There's no denying that. Their love for Christ and for each other, and their compassion for people are what make them so attractive to others. That's why I love them and count them as dear friends.

Right on, Maria!

—Nicky Cruz
Evangelist and Author

Generally people don't like change. Maria Durso's amazing personal journey and God's intervention reveals the extraordinary transformation available to us all who dare to believe in Jesus. This is a change everyone should welcome. It's not just good for you. It's also essential for a life of joy, hope, and love. When you read this book, you will learn how to find peace with God for yourself, and how to lead others to do so. This is a change you can live for.

—Commissioner James M. Knaggs
Territorial Commander, The Salvation Army

Maria is a unique person with a life story that will bring tears and a greater faith for what the Lord can do to change a person from the worst of circumstances to a miracle of grace transformation. This book will touch the lives of all who read it. Great job, Maria!

—Frank DaMazio
Lead Pastor, City Bible Church, Portland, Oregon

It has been said that emotion is the hinge of logic. Although we are wholly intellectual and logical creatures, deep change occurs when people get to our hearts. Maria Durso is masterful at getting to our hearts because she bravely opened up her heart to God and now to us in this wonderful work.

—David D. Ireland, PhD
Senior Pastor, Christ Church, Montclair, New Jersey
Author of *The Kneeling Warrior* (www.DavidIreland.org)

I have never met anyone who loves the voice of the Lord more than Maria Durso! Maria's devotion and dedication in worship and to the Word of God are contagious. The insights and revelation Maria finds in Scripture are so full of freedom and power that it is evident her time spent with the Lord produces deep wells of wisdom. There is a trust Maria carries from the Lord for the lost and broken that is rare and priceless. Maria's passion for redemption and wholeness is a literal gift to the body of Christ everywhere!

—Rita Springer
Worship Leader and Recording Artist

From the moment I read the introduction of this book authored by my dear friend Maria Durso, I knew it would be a powerful instrument for deep healing. Many people walk through this life unaware that they have a heart condition. They feel the effects, but they can't locate the cause.

In this amazing book you will go on a journey into the depths of your heart, and the adage "my heart has a mind of its own" will come alive to you.

You will discover things buried deep that will finally surface and be removed through the revelatory information within these pages. And when you have read the last line, you will find, as Maria did, that God is able to do exceedingly and abundantly above what you could ask or think!

—Carol Kornacki
Evangelist and Author

Maria is not only gifted with insight on church and family matters. Her spiritual insight and ability to communicate God's Word in a very practical and life-changing way will also bless every reader. She is gifted to teach each person how easy it is to not only know the Lord but also to walk with Him every day.

—Mary Colbert
Cofounder of Divine Health Ministries
Author of *13 Women You Should Never Marry*

Maria Durso has written a book that offers us the possibility of actualizing success in every area of our lives. She teaches that if we get our hearts right we can get everything right. And since Scripture does, in fact, intimate that the heart feels, reasons, understands, imagines, discerns right and wrong, and makes decisions, I couldn't agree more with the message of this book. Even more than the message, though, I am struck by the credibility of the messenger. Maria absolutely embodies this truth. She and her husband, Michael—who have led one of the great churches in New York City for more than thirty years—are dear friends and mentors to me and my wife, Sharon. I can affirm that Maria is a living testimony to this powerful message.

I highly recommend Maria and her wonderful book.

—Terry A. Smith
Lead Pastor, The Life Christian Church
West Orange, New Jersey
Author of *Live 10: Jump-Start the Best Version of Your Life*

Maria Durso passionately embodies the profound message in her new book. There is, indeed, a powerful, life-altering link between the heart and the head. In her book Maria articulates with anointing God's vision to bring about a fiery fusion between the heart and the head through the empowering enablement of the Holy Spirit. Every time I hear Maria share, I find my own heart aflame and my mind challenged and changed. For everyone who dares to pick up these pages and read them, I am sure they too will experience a heart and head revolution.

—Corey Jones
Lead Pastor, Crossroads Tabernacle, Fort Worth, Texas

If there was anyone I would trust with the absolute priority of moving the knowledge of God from head to heart it would be Maria Durso. I have stood next to her in Christ Tabernacle prayer meetings and heard her passionately cry out to God for the church and community. I watched her stand for years with unmovable faith for her three sons through some dark days until they became the men of God they are today. I have heard her stir the hearts of audiences of all ages with her life story and vibrant preaching. Maria has a heart ablaze for God, and I am confident the Holy Spirit will set your heart ablaze through the pages of this book.

—Alec Rowlands, DMin
Senior Pastor, Westgate Chapel, Edmonds, Washington
President of Church Awakening, Edmonds, Washington

DEDICATION

First and foremost, this book is dedicated to none other than the Holy
Spirit. For years when people said I should write a book, I always
responded by saying, "If God wants me to write a book, He will send a
publisher to me."

When I went to write the book, I was terrified and felt I needed a
ghostwriter. The Holy Spirit clearly spoke to me and said, "You don't need
a ghostwriter. You have the Holy Ghost writer." Sure enough, He has been
the source of all these revelations.

I'd also like to dedicate this book to all those who have struggled just
like me to truly believe in the deepest recesses of their hearts that they are
loved and valued by God. May they all make the eighteen-inch journey.

CONTENTS

ACKNOWLEDGMENTS

Above all I want to thank my amazing and most precious husband, Michael, who for almost forty years has always been my biggest cheerleader. Thank you, Michael, for gently sitting me down and urging me not to procrastinate any longer and reminding me that I was made for this. Thank you for patiently reading the chapters—all the chapters—over and over and over again. You are my greatest love and encourager.

To my amazing sons . . .

Adam, who would have thought that the little boy who said he wanted to be president would become one of the leading influencers of this generation, changing the face of youth ministry. You have also been a prophetic voice to speak to those who have the ability to influence. You are one of the most brilliant, insightful, and sensitive people I know.

Jordan, who would have thought the little boy who would never sleep in anyone's house would end up traveling to the four corners of the earth. You not only became God's representative in presidential palaces but also brought the gospel and humanitarian aid to the least of these. You are one of the most compassionate, merciful, and fearless people I know.

Chris, who would have thought the little boy who was diagnosed with ADHD and called stupid in the first grade by his teacher would write a revolutionary book and lead one of the most impactful youth and young adult ministries in the nation. God has propelled you to stand on the most coveted platforms around the world. You are one of the most tender, creative, and loving people I know.

Each one of you is a world-changer in your own right, and I know that for a fact, because you have changed my world. I am your greatest fan! Thank you for fanning into flame the gift of God within me. I cannot even imagine what the Lord has in store for all of you and Papa and Nana's grandbabies.

To my daughters-in-law, Lucy and Yahris—God gave my sons the most well-suited and priceless gift when He gave you to them. You were tailor-made to be a perfect fit for our family and the missing pieces of my heart.

To Ralph Castillo, my son in the Lord—who would have thought when you walked into our home as a young child you would have walked into our hearts. To me, you are the poster child for this book. Although the odds were against you, you took the eighteen-inch journey and became one of the godliest men and most brilliant communicators I know.

I want to thank my incredible assistant, Penny Mack, who is worth a million to me. I could never do without you. You tirelessly helped me with my research and stood by my side, supporting me every step of the way.

I want to thank Marie Armenia, who is an amazing author in her own right. You gave me a parade—marching band and all—after every rewrite. You could have definitely finished your own book with all the time you took with this one. Thank you, my friend.

To my precious Diana Denis, I watched you grow up, and grow up you did. You are so incredibly gifted, and you encouraged me to fulfill my calling. Thank you.

To Renee Fisher, your willingness and enthusiasm to see this book in print was a godsend. What an incredible gift you are to the Body of Christ and to me.

To the Intercessory Prayer Band at Christ Tabernacle, my fellow soldiers, and their "general," Brenda Finn, who have continually blown the wind of God behind me throughout the whole eighteen-inch journey—none of this would ever be possible without all of you. Last but not least, my family at Christ Tabernacle, who together have taken the eighteen-inch journey through every season for three decades. Pastoring alongside my husband has been my greatest joy. There is no place like home. I love you, and I need you. I love my church!

FOREWORD

Maria Durso is incredibly qualified to talk about the changes Jesus can make in a life. In fact, you could say she has a PhD on the subject! Her book, *From Your Head to Your Heart*, chronicles not only the startling change God made in her own life, but also the many valuable lessons she has learned—along with the way since that memorable day when she became a walking miracle.

Much of religion in the twenty-first century focuses only on facts about God, which I hope gets stored in our brains. But when it comes to experiencing the transforming power of Jesus Christ in a way that alters everything about us, that is another story altogether. God has raised up Maria to proclaim and teach about something much deeper than mental concepts about the Creator of the universe. She invites the reader to experience real change that comes from Someone who loves us more than we can imagine.

The word *change* intimidates or frightens many today since it always seems safer to stick with the status quo. But Maria Durso's new book calms all those fears as she explains the steps that will lead us to a peace-, joy-, and purpose-filled life beyond our wildest dreams. What makes it so powerful is that it all happened in her own life. She's not an author with a mere argument or doctrinal position. She knows personally that the distance between your head and your heart holds the secret that unlocks all the beautiful things a loving God has planned for your life. Read this carefully—meditate on its simple truths—and experience the same wonderful changes that God gave to Maria.

—Jim Cymbala
Senior Pastor
Brooklyn Tabernacle

INTRODUCTION

I became a Christian in 1975. I was saved from a very reckless and sinful past. As you will read in this book, I was instantly delivered from drug abuse, partying, and an immoral lifestyle the day I walked down the long aisle in church to give my life to Christ. My external sinful behaviors were immediately gone. But what was not as immediate was being delivered from years and years of low self-esteem. It would take decades for me to feel I was truly loved and accepted by God—that *I* had value and worth, and that a holy God could possibly use someone with a past like mine. I lived my life in turmoil and private agony. A battle raged within. I knew in my mind that Jesus loved me, "for the Bible tells me so." I knew in my mind that I was not an orphan, because God's Word tells me that I've been adopted and grafted into His family. But it would be years and years before that thinking would transfer into my heart.

I always felt like there was sludge between my head and my heart. I would have to fight through layers and layers of resistance before the truth could finally be transferred into my heart. The battle was intense. I read great books about the battlefield of the mind, but knowing something in your head and knowing it in your heart are worlds apart. Being assured in your heart that you are loved is a far cry from just knowing it in your head. Trusting someone in your head and trusting someone in your heart is as different as knowing someone as an acquaintance and having that person as your best friend. Knowing in your heart is the game changer. Your heart seals the deal.

It has been said that there is a distance of eighteen inches between the head and the heart—a separation of a foot and a half. When I look back, I realize I was oftentimes just eighteen inches from victory. Only eighteen inches of steep terrain needed to be conquered. The distance of eighteen inches may seem short, but the road is extremely long and winding. Yet this distance can definitely be shortened and the road made much less turbulent when we make a vital connection.

In 1991 Dr. J. Andrew Armour introduced the idea that the heart has its own brain. In his book *Neurocardiology* Armour revealed that the heart "has an elaborate circuitry that allows it to act independently of the cranial brain—to learn, remember, even sense and feel."[1] *Ah!* This extremely important information would confirm what I had felt all these years—and prove that I wasn't a weirdo! I also realized that if this was, in fact, true, then number one, the Bible would confirm it (because science will ultimately prove what God has written in His Word). Number two, I wouldn't be the only one sensing this deep divide on the inside.

According to the research, the brain in the head is connected to the brain in the heart. The two brains send messages to each other through thousands of neurons and tiny filaments, but the messages don't necessarily coincide.[2] To us laymen this may seem to be just some boring medical information that has nothing to do with us or our spiritual life. But I assure you it has everything to do with us. This affects every facet of our lives, especially our spiritual life.

Think about the reality behind this truth. Don't we oftentimes say things like, "My mind is telling me one thing, but my heart is saying something else"? This is why our behaviors often are out of sync with what we profess to believe. No bona fide, born-again Christian would dare read the Word and say outright, "Well, I really don't believe that," or, "I think God is a liar because what I feel doesn't match up at all with what I read." *Never!* This is why many times we can hear a sermon, walk out of church believing that we can scale a wall, truly know that God's Word is yea and amen, and yet a week later find that the excitement behind that life-changing truth has fizzled out. It's as though the revelation thief stole the faith we had to live out the truth we received.

I don't think the problem was with our ability to believe the truth in our minds. I believe that as the truth was working its way down into our heart, it was suddenly rejected and expelled by the heart's brain because of some fear and past experience. We had a heart attack of sorts. The heart is the seat of our emotions, not the mind. It's where all the action in our lives takes place. The Bible says in Proverbs 23:7 that as a man *thinks in his heart, so is he*. It doesn't say as a man thinks *in his head*. Proverbs 3:5 says, "Trust in the Lord with *all your heart*, and lean not on your own understanding" (nkjv, emphasis added). It doesn't say, "Trust in the Lord with *all your head*"! The Bible clearly differentiates between the head and the heart. Psalm 26:2 says, "Examine me, O Lord, and prove me; try *my mind* and *my heart*" (nkjv, emphasis added).

Although the battle in our minds is very real, I don't think we can ignore this other battlefront that must be won in the heart. The war raging in the mind is only half the battle. The heart's brain must be healed from all the years of disappointment and rejection. We need God to heal our broken hearts—or shall we say the broken way our hearts think!

I believe we are just eighteen inches from victory, and just as a firefighter identifies the source of a fire in the midst of ruins, so can we start to identify the hotspots from where the battle rages and ask God to heal them. My prayer is that this book would be like a long-awaited prescription, and that when you finish reading these pages, healing would start to flow. I believe that after we identify these vulnerable places—these "hotspots"—God will be able to give us the "brain wash" needed to heal the hemorrhaging brain in our hearts. So let's start to take the eighteen-inch trek from our heads all the way down into the deep valley of our hearts, so we can slay the giants that are defying God's promises and blocking our blessings!

CHAPTER 1 – THE GREATEST DISTORTER OF REVELATION

If you ever look back to try to figure out why you are the way you are, I'm sure you'll identify specific moments that were accompanied by specific words that shaped your thinking. Those words may even seem to have taken on a life of their own. Words, whether positive or negative, can affect the course of our lives. The Bible says in Proverbs 18:21, "The tongue has the power of life and death." No truer words have been spoken (no pun intended). Words can either bury us or resurrect us.

As words roll off the tongue, they act as a sharpened pen that writes deeply on the tablets of our heart. Words can write into us confidence or failure. Words write the script long before we step onto life's stage and find ourselves acting out the drama, because words precede actions. Words spoken to us in the past often sign off on our future. Such was my experience. It seemed that almost everything that happened to me just confirmed that what I was told as a child was true.

It is a fact—a scientific fact—that words spoken to us are etched deeply into the memory of the heart's brain. As I said in the introduction, scientists have recently confirmed what was written in the Bible thousands of years ago. They discovered that the heart actually has its own brain. It has the capacity to think and store memory. The Word declares that as a man thinks *in his heart*, so is he (Prov. 23:7). In other words, the thoughts imprinted in the brain of the heart, which came from words previously spoken to us, direct the way we view life and the way we think about ourselves. Those words can be so attached to who we think we are, it can seem next to impossible to believe otherwise.

The negative assaults launched slowly at our hearts since our childhood are like mini "heart attacks" on the brains of our hearts, and they have shaped the way we view life. This "heart brain" is where our feelings, or our emotions, are formed. Our emotions are the place from which most of us view life. So is it safe to say that feelings are the greatest distorter of revelation. Our emotions oftentimes hide the truth of God's Word. So even though you want to believe what the Bible says, it's as though there is a blockage in the brain of your heart. You then suffer from unnecessary anguish.

Could you then say your heart is broken? Technically the brain of your heart is broken. But God says in His Word that He will bind up the broken heart. God wants to come along and serve as a surgeon who makes those broken places whole. As our Great Physician, the Holy Spirit wants to mend our hearts until they are totally transformed and functioning as He intended. He wants to not only rewrite our future but also use our past to help others.

When I was a little girl, religious women told me that I didn't have a mother because *God didn't think I deserved* one! The words "you don't deserve" or "God doesn't think you deserve" are the ones that have shaped most of my life. Those words became imprinted in the depths of my being. Those words—an opinion—formed who I thought I was and my feelings about the way God felt about me. I couldn't enjoy amazing opportunities when they came along because I didn't think I deserved them. I would purposely sabotage them, putting myself down and talking myself out of them, all because my innermost being shouted, "You don't deserve it!" Back then I would rather *not* try, than try and see what I felt was true become a reality. I've often said that great things can happen *to you* and *for you*, but if it doesn't happen *in you*, then the way you view yourself won't change. We are led by our hearts or, rather, the brains in our hearts.

Our whole Christian faith is about believing that we are loved by God. We, as messed up as we are, are unconditionally loved by this all-loving God, and He alone can change us from the inside out and conform us into His image and likeness. That's the gospel, the good news . . . no, allow me to correct myself . . . the *great news*! Now, without this belief system being firmly fixed in place, our foundation is very shaky. No, let me correct myself again . . . it's more than shaky—it makes our faith so weak that it can be blown down at any moment by the slightest hint of someone's disapproval. It will leave us living in fear that God is displeased with us. We become fearful of making a mistake, fearful of being judged or criticized, and profoundly fearful of failure. So we procrastinate stepping out in faith and doing what God calls us to do, not because we don't love God but because we fear He really doesn't love us.

That is what happened to me. Oh, I knew that God loved *you*, but I really didn't believe He truly loved *me*. When I put my head on the pillow at night, I was never sure that I had done enough. I lived under constant accusation and guilt. I would hear voices in my head that said: "If you really loved God, you would have prayed for two hours. If you really loved God, you would have put *all* your money in the offering. If you really loved God, you would have driven Sister So-and-So to Timbuktu!" So then, beneath the weight of this heavy load, I spent all my efforts trying to gain God's approval instead of resting in the knowledge that I already have His approval and because of it I can breathe and live for Him—and so can you.

A Living Nightmare

My mother and father were in the nightclub business. My dad owned a club in Manhattan, and my mom was a nightclub singer. After some years together they desperately wanted to have a baby. Finally, after years of trying, my twenty-nine-year-old mom became pregnant. It was 1950. From the beginning of her pregnancy she experienced horrible headaches. There was no such a thing as an MRI or a CAT scan back then. The doctors said they were just headaches caused by the pregnancy and that they would dissipate after the first trimester.

But the headaches didn't cease, and one day when my mom was five months pregnant, my dad came home to find her with a towel wrapped around her head. She was banging her head against the wall trying to find some relief from the pain. She was in excruciating pain. She was rushed to the hospital. The doctors told my dad that she had an inoperable brain tumor. At the hospital she slipped into a coma, and the doctors opened her up and delivered a two-and-a-half-pound baby girl. My mom never had a chance to see me or hold me.

The day my mother died was the day my father died. Although he was physically breathing, he wasn't alive. He lost the love of his life, and a baby, a pre-mature baby, was certainly no replacement or consolation. Because my dad checked out, I was brought to the New York Foundling Hospital, where they place orphans. I had no name on my birth certificate. No one bothered to name me because no one expected me to live. What were the odds of surviving at that birth weight in those days? God must have had a plan!

A nurse named me Maria after I had been hospitalized for eight months. Instead of wasting away, I continued to grow and I got stronger. When I was healthy enough, my dad finally came to take me home, but what would this man do with a baby girl? "Single parent" was not even a term back then. I believed my dad did the best he could with the deck he had been dealt, but he definitely suffered from depression, although depression wasn't readily diagnosed or understood in those days. My memories are of him looking out our Manhattan apartment window with a cigarette and a glass of scotch in his hand, crying for my mother. My dad never said as much, but I grew up thinking that I gave her a cancerous brain tumor and that if she hadn't gotten pregnant with me, she would still be alive.

When I was almost three years old, my dad enrolled me in a religious boarding school. He felt my needs would be met there. There were no women in my life and He believed I would bond with women there. My dad didn't have the wherewithal to feed me and at the school I would be given three square meals a day. He also believed that my educational and spiritual needs would be met. I remember the day he drove me down the long gravel road and parked in front of this huge edifice. The doors seemed to be hundreds of feet high. As I held my little suitcase in hand, my dad bent down and said to me, "Maria, this is the best thing for the both of us, and I will come and visit you when I can." But his visits were very few and far between.

A woman dressed in black from head to toe answered the door and escorted me inside. I heard the door slam behind me. The place was cold and, I would learn, void of love. The place that was supposed to be the answer to my needs became everything but. It was in this place where my nightmare began.

The nuns beat me on a regular basis. They pulled chunks of hair out of my head and punched me in the face. I was made to place my hands in an open desk, and the top would be slammed down on them. I would be awakened in the middle of the night and placed in a dark, cold stairway. Because I'm left-handed, I was told that the devil lived inside of me. So I would be placed in a bathtub of scalding hot water to get the devil out of me.

In the summer, when all the other girls went home, I didn't. I would be molested. I was given a glass of muscatel wine to make me drowsy, and then I'd wake up in someone else's bed. But worse than any physical or sexual abuse was the emotional abuse I endured. This is where I heard the dreaded sentence that caused me to think I was a loser and that this life sentence came from the hand of God. "Maria," I was told, "you don't have a mother because *God* didn't think you *deserved one!*"

The other little girls went home every weekend and came back with cards from their mommies and daddies. Their suitcases smelled like what I imagined love to smell like. But even more than the cards and the sweet fragrance, the thing I wanted most of all was the lipstick mark they wore on their cheeks. That was the seal. It meant, "Don't worry. I'll be back for you next week." It meant they were protected. No one would dare lay a hand on them. They were special, and they knew it. But I wasn't. It was as simple as that!

Now I think that maybe, just maybe, someone should have seen my life as a miracle that needed to be nurtured and tended to. Maybe, just maybe, God loved me and had such a purpose for my life that He intervened and caused that doctor to open my mom up and preserve my life. Maybe, just maybe, not being born or brought up under normal circumstances doesn't have to mean that you're odd or a misfit. Maybe, just maybe, the presence of trials doesn't mean the absence of God. But because I was told the opposite, I was always chasing after that lipstick mark to feel approved, and the approval I was seeking was something I would never have—not with man anyway!

A Profound Revelation

I had a profound experience many years ago that shed light on the crux of my issues. I had been saved for about fifteen years at the time, and I was already at Christ Tabernacle, the church my husband and I pastor. Christ Tabernacle is the first church to be birthed out of the Brooklyn Tabernacle, which is the church where I first experienced God's presence and learned about faith and prayer. So you can imagine how honored and elated I was when I was asked to be a speaker at their very first women's retreat. I immediately went to the Lord, and if I remember correctly, my prayer went something like, "Lord, I need a word from heaven" (which really wasn't necessary to pray. After all, where else would He give me a word from? Definitely not the other place!). I was looking for something profound. I continued, "Lord, this is the Brooklyn Tabernacle. I need a word [organ playing in the background]. Lord, please help me. It has to be deep. Show me who the Antichrist is, the 666, something from the Book of Revelation—anything. I need to impress them!"

I know you're probably thinking, "What an awful, self- centered prayer." It definitely was. Well, needless to say God didn't answer that prayer. As the time came closer for me to speak, I was in a panic because I had heard nothing from the Holy Spirit. Then one morning—one life-changing morning—I finally heard Him speak as I was making my bed. As I threw my comforter in the air to fluff it up, I distinctly heard the Holy Spirit say, "I want you to ask them, *Do you believe God really loves you?*" I said, "*What?* You want me to ask them that, Lord? Are You kidding me? Don't You know the song, 'Jesus loves me this I know, for the Bible tells me so'? Lord, that is so basic. How in the world am I going to stand up in front of the women at the Brooklyn Tabernacle and ask them such a childish question?"

Then I heard the question that changed my life. The Holy Spirit asked me, "Maria, do *you* believe that I really love you?" I thought about it for a quick second and started to weep profusely. Oh, I believed He loved others, but *me?* I had to admit to myself that I didn't believe Jesus really loved me. I knew *in my head* that He loved me, but I realized that I truly didn't believe in my heart that He loved me. I was eighteen inches—a foot and a half—from victory.

This was where my deep issues had their root, from where all my trust issues stemmed. The Holy Spirit neatly wrapped up every feeling of insecurity, worthlessness, and fear in an instant and narrowed it down for me by identifying my double-mindedness. The belief that God loves us is the critical truth on which the rest of our faith hinges. The failure to believe this is the difference between living our life trying to gain God's approval and living our life knowing that we already have His approval.

Think about it this way: Imagine two choirs singing. Everyone is singing the same song, swaying in the same direction, but there is a major difference. As one group sings, they are crying out in the depths of their being, "Lord, I'm singing. Do You love me now?" As the other group is singing, they're saying within, "Because He loves me, I sing." In church we are all doing the same thing outwardly, but the issue is not what we are doing. The issue is *why* we are doing what we are doing!

When we don't believe we are loved—in our hearts—we never feel like we've done enough. There is no rest, no enjoyment of God's presence. We definitely need our hearts to experience a brain wash to cleanse away all the false impressions we have of God. That day in that room as I was making my bed and had a meltdown, the Holy Spirit directed me to open my Bible, and He gave me a simple illustration concerning Mary of Bethany. I realize that what He showed me that day may not be chronologically correct; nevertheless, that revelation was not only the beginning of my mind and heart being transformed, but it has set many on a path of healing. The picture He gave me was crystal clear.

In Luke 10:38–42 Mary is *sitting* at Jesus's feet—and *she is empty-handed.* Her sister, Martha, comes out of the kitchen like a lunatic *accusing* her sister of leaving her to do all the work. Martha represents *family*—those close to us. What does Jesus do? *He defends Mary!*

In John 12:1–8 the Bible says it's six days before the Passover, and "Mary took about a pint of pure nard, an expensive perfume; she poured it on Jesus' feet and wiped his feet with her hair" (v. 3). Judas speaks up and *accuses* Mary of being wasteful. This perfume could have been sold and the money given to the poor, he says. Judas represents *the enemy*. What does Jesus do? *He defends her!*

In Mark 14:3–9 the Bible says it's two days before the Passover, and Mary "broke the jar and poured the perfume on [Jesus's] head." The disciples *accused* her and rebuked her harshly. *Wow!* Anyone see a pattern? The disciples represent our brothers and sisters in Christ. What does Jesus do? *He defends her!*

Looking at this simple illustration, allow me to share two simple thoughts. First, let's notice Mary's body language as she gets to know Jesus. At first she is sitting at His feet but not touching Him. Then she is pouring "just about a pint" of perfume while actually *touching His feet*. Next she is *breaking the bottle* and has worked her way up to His head, His face, eye to eye. She could now feel His breath on her. This is intimacy!

Here we have one of the vital keys to making strides in reducing the eighteen inches between our heads and our hearts. Here we see clearly the progression of surrender. Surrender isn't instant; it's progressive.

Surrender is a pint at a time!

Second, notice that in every instance as she tried to gain ground and get closer to Jesus, she was *accused*. The accusations came from familiar voices—her family, the enemy, and the "church" brethren. But in every instance, *Jesus defended her!* It was only when she saw Jesus as her *defender* and not her *accuser* that she was able to trust Him and thus *surrender* her most valued possession.

Ladies and gentlemen, Jesus is our defender. He is not our accuser.

Don't allow those voices of accusation to keep you from getting to Jesus any longer. Know that when you take a daring step forward, you will face opposition, but *it won't be from Him!* The Bible tells us, "For the accuser of our brothers and sisters, who accuses them before our God day and night, has been hurled down. They triumphed over him by the *blood of the Lamb* and by *the word of their testimony*" (Rev. 12:10–11, emphasis added).

What is the word of our testimony? It is that we are unconditionally loved by God, and if God loved us enough to save us, then who are we to argue with Him? I believe it's time to wash the brains of our hearts, or should I say, it's time for us to get a much-needed brain wash. We are just eighteen inches from victory. Come on, it may be a pint at a time, but eventually the bottle of fear, worthlessness, and insecurity will be emptied out. As we trust God in the deepest recesses of our being and grow in the profound knowledge of His love, the Holy Spirit will enable us to surrender our most private pain and our most intimate dreams.

He's our defender, not our accuser!

Let's Pray

Let's ask God today for the grace to see that He is our defender. Make your prayer personal.

Holy Spirit, reveal to me that You are my defender, not my accuser. As You reveal this truth to me, please start to wash my heart and lift all the residue of the past. I believe that as I absorb the depth of this heart-healing truth, I will make progress, and the distance between my head and heart will definitely be shortened. In Jesus's name, amen.

Maria Durso

CHAPTER 2 – WE NEED A BRAIN WASH

Let's go back for a moment to the mind-blowing scientific find that the heart has its own brain. Since now we know the heart has the ability to think, it stands to reason that the heart's brain has a memory bank. Years of memories have been deposited into the bank of your heart's brain. The brain in the heart has full capacity to remember. This is proven by the fact that some people who receive heart transplants start to have cravings they never had before and even have dreams related to the person whose heart they received.[1]

The heart is more than an organ that pumps blood; it also pumps past memories into our everyday life. Years of emotional data are locked up in the heart, and that is what makes it difficult to believe something that is contrary to your own personal experience. If you have been told something your whole life, even though it wasn't true, you are most likely to rely on what you've been told over and over again. Repetition is a surefire way to get you to believe something, because memories of the emotional experiences you've had again and again get lodged in your heart's brain.

With all this biblical information, would you not think that we need not only a thorough transformation of the mind but also a complete renovation of the heart? We need to be cleansed from top to bottom—eighteen inches of complete cleansing. We need both of our brains to be washed by God's Word so they can be in sync with His will.

I believe that's what happened to the Israelites who went out to scout the land in Numbers chapter 13. The people of God received the word of God, and they were going in to check out the Promised Land. This was Israel's shining moment, history in the making. The Israelites were about to fulfill their destiny. The very reason they were brought out of Egypt was to be brought into the land of promise. Isn't that the reason God brought us out of the slavery of this world? To bring us into a new land!

The Israelites exited Egypt to gain entrance into the Promised Land. I totally believe they were gung ho—sick and tired of being oppressed and ready to take over this new territory. There was no doubt in their minds that they would gain the victory. They sent in their baddest and brightest, the Navy SEALs of their day, the leaders, the heads of the tribes. And they came back with fruit so huge they had to carry it on their shoulders. This was concrete proof that what God said was true. They confirmed that the land absolutely did flow with milk and honey, and there was no record of anyone chasing them. No one in the land seemed to have any beef with them. As a matter of fact, Rahab the prostitute said, "I know that the Lord has given you this land and that a great fear of you has fallen on us" (Josh. 2:9).

Wow! Their enemies were practically wetting their tunics and shaking in their sandals! They also reported that the land was fertile just as God had promised. Yet they came back with fruit in hand and fear in their hearts. Fear so enveloped them that they were sure God was setting them up to fail. They acknowledged the fruit was huge and the land was fertile, but they said the people were stronger and the land was too large to conquer. They said in essence what we so often feel way down deep in our hearts: "We can't change our culture. The giant of culture is greater than God. We can't stand for righteousness; our God is no match for those giants." Then they declared these famous words: "We seem as grasshoppers in our own eyes and so we were in theirs." (See Numbers 13:33.) Look at the way the New Century Version puts it: "We felt like grasshoppers, and we looked like grasshoppers to them." Where do those feelings come from? Our emotions—our heart!

In my opinion, God's people suffered from "grasshopper-itis," or as I also like to refer to it, the "grasshopper sin-drome." The Israelites' enemy wasn't on the outside; it was on the inside. It wasn't the giants in the land that threatened to defeat them; it was the giant of low self-image and self-worth. After all, their whole lives they were the underdogs. They weren't conquerors; they were slaves, the lowest on the totem pole. So it stands to reason that their past was present with them.

Along with the fruit they were carrying on their shoulders, they were also carrying around a gigantic sense of fruitlessness. They were experiencing a tug-of-war between the two brains. I can picture the battle. Their minds were confirming what God said, but their hearts were fighting tooth and nail to keep them steady—and stuck. Their sense of defeat had nothing to do with the five-hundred-mile round-trip journey they had just taken; it had everything to do with the eighteen-inch journey they still needed to take. What they knew to be true in their heads and what they saw with their own eyes couldn't stand up to what they felt in their own hearts.

Truth be told, the walk to the Promised Land isn't horizontal; it's vertical. A low concept of God will not only destroy our God-given potential, but it will also destroy a city, which in turn will ruin a nation. Before we can venture out and change our city, we must conquer the territory of the heart; that is the first and most important leg of the journey. The Israelites were just eighteen inches from victory—so close but so far.

It's amazing that how we see ourselves is the way we think everybody sees us, and the way we feel becomes our reality. The things we go through in life shapes the view we have of ourselves and often cause us to limit ourselves. This is why we need the brains in our hearts to be thoroughly washed. Yes, as I've stated previously, we need a brain wash so we can see ourselves the way God sees us and reach our potential.

Oh, I know the sin-drome all too well! I'm an expert in diagnosing this plague. I'd been infected with this dreaded disease for as long as I could remember. I truly used to think that God was setting me up to fail. I thought if you liked me, there was something wrong with you. How could *you* like *me*? *I* didn't like me! Every time I went out to speak at a conference, I would notice the one person sleeping instead of the hundreds who were alert. Or I would be sure to get in the elevator with someone who reminded me that I sounded like Valerie Harper's character Rhoda on *The Mary Tyler Moore Show*. Or some so-called Bible scholar would come and tell me what Bible fact I should have included in my sermon.

I had someone tell me once that I exaggerate the Word, that I'm a show-off, and that I'm too loud. At one time comments like that would have nearly destroyed me. Because of the view I had of myself, my frailties and vulnerabilities became the enemy's target. Of course, these accusations always came from respectable religious people—people like the ones in that boarding school, women who hadn't lived the sinful life I had lived or done the things I had done. And those women were always sure to let me know that I wasn't as good and pure as they were.

I remember as a little girl going to camp for just one summer. I had the kindest, most beautiful camp counselor ever. I'll call her Miss B. I will never, ever forget her kindness to me. She placed my cot next to her bed at night, and she really tried to build me up. But because of what happened to me during the summer months in the boarding school, it wasn't easy to accept this outpouring of love from Miss B. I was always wondering why she was being so nice to me. Was she going to molest me too? Would I wake up in bed with her, the same way I woke up other times before?

Every year, as was the tradition in this camp, they would pick a "Queen for the Day." One queen was chosen from each age group. I was probably four or five years old at the time. Each camper from each group would have to pick a card, and the one who chose the queen of hearts was the winner. When Miss B got to me, she let the card slip just enough for me to see what it was. She looked at me and then down at the card. Again and again she looked at me and then at the card. She was practically placing it in my hand. Miss B wanted me to be Queen for the Day.

Thoughts swirled in my mind. I was going to be given a crown and a cape, and I could eat ice cream and not the usual liver or thick slice of fatty ham. Plus, someone would clean my space in the cabin. But then the words "You don't deserve to be Queen for the Day" started to scream from within. My mind was saying one thing—"Go ahead, pick the card; this is your big chance"— but *my heart* was confirming what had been my reality. I was the little girl who didn't have a mother because *God* didn't think I deserved one. If God didn't think enough of me to let me have a mother, then how could I think well enough of myself to be Queen for the Day?

I agreed, as I always did, with that voice within, and I chose another card. It was so much easier to live the way I always had than to become someone different, someone significant. I believe I saw a tear fall from Miss B's eye. I had not thought of that story for many, many years, but one day as I was speaking at a conference, the Holy Spirit suddenly brought it to mind. As I was recounting the event, a woman got out of her seat, walked down the aisle, interrupted the meeting, and handed me a card. It was the queen of hearts! I was stunned—dumbfounded!

She said as she was leaving to come to the conference, the Holy Spirit told her to go back into the house and get the queen of hearts out of a deck of cards she had in the house. She said, *"What?* Come on, Lord. That's so odd."* But the impression was so strong that she just couldn't ignore it. When she handed me that card in front of all those people at that church in North Carolina, I fell to my knees and started to weep. That God would remember the turmoil I endured that day and affirm me in front of those women was a very hard concept for me to grasp.

I've had amazing things happen to me throughout the years-amazing things orchestrated by God alone. I believe we see many people holding a mic and standing on a platform that are doing it by total faith—feelings have nothing to do with it. I was on *100 Huntley Street*, a Christian TV show in Canada, and the makeup artist said, "I've never seen anyone as nervous as you." I explained that I wished I could run away. I didn't want to be on TV. I didn't want people to stare at me and possibly pick me apart. Then came the time for me to walk out onto to the set. They sat me on a beautiful couch, and the gorgeous host started to interview me. The Holy Spirit moved in such an incredible way that as I was walking off the set, the host said, "The Holy Spirit is in this place; the Holy Spirit is in this place!" The network's telephones were ringing off the hook. The host motioned for me to come back on the set. They canceled the next guest and continued to talk with me. They said that had never happened in the history of the show.

I've been invited to speak in denominations that have never had a woman speak to men—God has done some truly amazing things. But I've come to realize that although great things happen to you, they won't change you. The change has to happen in you! Even though God opened these incredible doors of ministry that I carefully walked through, I still needed a thorough cleansing to change how I viewed myself in my heart.

A Grasshopper Mentality

I did a small study on grasshoppers from the encyclopedia. It is amazing how there is not one random word in Scripture. The symbolism is just amazing. Allow me to give you some grasshopper facts and see if you see the same parallels I'm seeing:

- Fact #1: Grasshoppers travel in large numbers with other grasshoppers but have absolutely no purpose. Scientists are baffled by their very existence. Because they travel in such large numbers, they obscure the sun and hide its light.
- Fact #2: Grasshoppers are destructive; they ravage the land without replenishing it or contributing to it in any way.
- Fact #3: Grasshoppers have an unusual habit of eating one another instead of eating other insects. In other words, they eat their own kind.
- Fact #4: Grasshoppers are the chief target or prey of other insects and reptiles.
- Fact #5: When being attacked, instead of fighting back by using their strong jaws to bite or their amazing ability to jump onto higher ground, they usually exhibit no movement at all. They blend into their surroundings, frozen in fear.[2]

Can you see the typology in this? When we have a grasshopper mentality, we are relatively useless and purposeless. We travel in large numbers but have no real effect on our world, except maybe to tear down the places we visit instead of replenishing the land. Oftentimes we obscure the Son and hide the light of God's presence. We tend to bite and devour one another instead of attacking the real enemy. When we are attacked, we blend in or do nothing instead of jumping to higher ground or using God's Word to take a bite out of the enemy's lies.

But of all the traits of grasshoppers, this is the kicker. All types of filthy flies, full of bacteria, lay their eggs and hatch their young on the backs of grasshoppers. The baby flies eat their way through the eggshell, eating the grasshopper alive in the process, and the grasshopper just sits there and allows it to happen.[3] Is that not just like the devil, who plants lies on our backs that hatch and then eat us alive—and we allow it to happen!

I had an incredible revelation one day. I bought my home in 1978. It's a good, sturdy house, but there was always one chronic issue: a leak in my dining room that came from the shower above. For years I had all sorts of experts tell me how to fix the problem. "It's the grout," they'd say, so we would replace the grout. For a time it seemed to fix the problem, but eventually the stain of the water would bleed through. "It's the fixtures," we were told, so we bought new fixtures. Again it seemed to be the answer for a time, but after a while again the dreaded stain on the ceiling. "It's the tile," we were told. "It's the lead pan." So in compliance with the experts' advice, we broke up the new tile and put in a new lead pan. Again the stain. "The lead pan isn't tipped right," we were told, so we had to break up the shower floor yet again to tip the lead pan to the perfect angle. *Ugh!* All the while, the ceiling in my dining room was being patched, repatched, scraped, taped, and painted to no avail.

Finally we inherited some money, so we decided to put in a brand-new, desperately needed bathroom. *Hooray!* This would certainly solve our chronic problem. So we hired a contractor to draw up plans, which involved removing the bathtub and replacing it with the shower of our dreams! This huge shower came equipped with all these different types of shower heads. It was almost like a water park! Our problem was finally solved. Then one day while strolling through my dining room, I just happened to look up to the ceiling, and lo and behold the dreaded stain was back. *No!* It just can't be. No way! How could this possibly happen?

I immediately called the bathroom remodelers, and they advised me to call Roto-Rooter. You know the jingle, "And away goes trouble down the drain"! They snaked our drains. "That should solve your problem, ma'am," I was told as my whole savings account went down the drain. The plumber also added a bit of advice. He said, "I don't think you should use all the shower heads at the same time. As a matter of fact, I will lower your water pressure." So now, when we went to take a shower, it took an hour to get wet. When someone was in the shower, we would yell, "Are you wet yet?" But we were willing to do whatever it took to solve our ongoing, annoying problem.

But a few months later, yes, you guessed it, not only a stain but a full-on leak! Water came pouring into my dining room, leaving the ceiling opened wide. The plumbing company sent over Hans the plumber. This time Hans decided that instead of working from the top down, he would work from the bottom up. He cleaned away the remaining debris, fully opening my ceiling. As I stood in my dining room, I noticed something life-changing. The new pipes from my shower were connected to the old pipes. The water would run easily through the new pipes, but would be met with opposition when it encountered the old pipes, thus creating a backup and then a leak. It turns out that the old pipes were filled with a thick sludge that basically formed a wall of cement. I realized that the leak would be a recurring problem unless the old pipes were cleaned through and through. It was never the grout or the lead pan or the fixtures. The problem was always the *old pipes!* Oh, what a revelation I had that day!

You see, when we are born again, we are given new life—new pipes, if you will. Didn't God say, "I will give you a new heart and put a new spirit in you" (Ezek. 36:26)? In verse 25, just one verse up, God explains how this process will take place. He says this will be done by sprinkling clean water on you (and we know that the clean water is symbolic of His Word that cleanses us thoroughly). Then He declares, "I will cleanse you from all your impurities and from all your idols," and when He does, "you will be clean" (v. 25).

God promises to wash us clean. His Word is able to invade all the sludge and gunk of the past. When we let His Word invade our hearts, it will clean away all the junk. The way for this process to be most effective is to live beneath that glorious, cleansing, life-giving fountain. Life comes from living underneath those effervescent sprinklers, drinking in and bathing in God's Word, allowing it to cleanse us to the uttermost. We *must* come to terms with the fact that it's to our benefit to "get into the Word" so that the Word can "get into us"—every part of us. The Word fairy, as much as I once wished there were such a creature, isn't going to sprinkle Word dust on us as we go on our merry way living in the sewers of the world.

So far so good, but what happens when those cleansing waters are met with opposition, i.e., the sludge of our old thinking—a wall of impenetrable cement that resists the Word of God? What happens when there's a kink in the sprinkling system? Our heart's brain, which is connected to our old way of thinking, has been the boss forever—and therein lies the kink, the blockage to our freedom! Our emotions have had the run of the house for all these years, and they don't like the new connection, especially since it involves change on our end.

So when my new mind, or my new "pipes," declare, "I can do *all* things through Christ who gives me strength" (see Philippians 4:13), my old pipes say, "*Really?* Not so fast, missy." The old Maria doesn't think she likes all this faith stuff. The old Maria doesn't really believe this new data, not way down deep in her heart. The old Maria, deep down inside, is afraid to trust in the Lord with *all her* heart. She is used to leaning on her own understanding. (See Proverbs 3:5.) But now God's Word is telling her to go in the opposite direction and *lean not on her own understanding* but in *all her ways*—all means all—*acknowledge Him* (Prov. 3:6)!

She's afraid to trust totally. What if she fails or falls? Leaning on God instead of leaning on self would take a changing of the guards, a relinquishing of power. But she likes to stay in control. It feels safe. Thus a tug-of-war ensues—and inevitably there's a leak! Unfortunately most of us would rather sand, paint, and gloss over our issues over and over again. Truth be told, if the old pipes aren't thoroughly cleansed and kept in line with God's Word, the revelation that God continually longs to give us through His Word will just keep being wasted—leaked out, if you will. We will keep on going around the same old mountain, fighting the same old enemies.

Who Are You, Really?

So who are you, and what are you thinking? Whatever you think in your heart is who you really are. That's why the brain in the heart, along with the brain in the head, needs a continual spiritual Roto-Rooter—an eighteen-inch brain wash from top to bottom and from bottom to top! The Bible says in Colossians 3:16, "Let the Word of Christ . . . have the run of the house" (The Message). Yes, God's Word should be running rampant throughout all the cracks and crevices of our "house," which is our inner man. I should in no way, shape, or form be running the Word of Christ out of my house! It would literally make a world of a difference if we would just allow the water of God's Word to penetrate and thoroughly renovate those hard places until we say with faith, "Yes, absolutely, no doubt about it, I can do all things through Christ who gives me strength—all because I'm in Christ and He's in me!"

Just as when waves continually dash against the rocks and they smooth all the rough edges, so you must flood the brain in your head and the brain in your heart with the promises of God until there is a complete and utter breakthrough. You must meditate on God's crystallized, perfect, pure Word. Oh, may the meditations of my *heart* be pleasing to Him. (See Psalm 19:14.) As we continually meditate on Him, His thoughts will transform our thoughts, producing right thinking within us.

His Word, which is basically His thoughts on paper, *must* win this tug-of-war and bring down the proponent of oppositional thinking. The Word, which has the strength of a hammer, must continually dash against the rocky places, washing away all the weeds, boulders, and thorny places, crushing the way the brains in our hearts are used to thinking. As God's Word continually soaks us, it will soften us, making supple and pliable all those rock-hard, resistant places. Then the Lord will be able to write on the tablets of our heart what He truly thinks about us. We must ask God for the grace to hold on to the promises and stand our ground so as not to allow a backup or a leak.

I want to end this chapter with a somewhat humorous story. Many years ago when we first started Christ Tabernacle, a woman who had gotten saved in our church asked to meet with me. I had noticed for the past few months that she had radically changed her dress. She went from someone who was once very stylish to someone who dressed very drab. She once wore makeup and cut her hair in cute styles, but now she appeared very matronly. As we sat down for the meeting, she told me how our church was good for beginners, but she needed the deeper things of God. She had found a church where she would get this kind of teaching. She needed a church that stripped the flesh of any opportunity to look attractive.

My heart sank to the ground. *Deeper?* What did she mean by *deeper?* She left our church, but those words didn't leave me. This was just another arrow to remind me that we weren't up to snuff! Every weekend I would ask my husband, "What are you going to speak about?" And God forbid he said the subject was love! *"Love?"* I would say. "Can't you speak about anything deeper than love?" Even though the Bible says there is no greater command than that we love others . . . but what does the Bible know? (I'm joking, of course.)

Many years passed without me seeing the woman, but make no mistake about it, she was sitting on the pew right by my side every Sunday. I judged every sermon by her remarks. Was it *deep*? One Sunday afternoon after church my husband and I were in a restaurant. Well, guess who was coming to dinner? Yep, you guessed it, Miss Deeper. I noted from afar that she looked different. She looked really pretty. As the Lord would have it, the waiter sat her and her date right next to me and my husband. She quickly said hi, but her boyfriend went straightaway to use the restroom. After he'd left, she turned to us and hurriedly said, "Please don't mention anything about church because he's not a Christian and I really like him."

Everything inside of me wanted to get up and take my plate of food and place it, gently of course, on Miss Deeper's head! I thought, "I can't believe her words crippled me for all these years and she's not even serving the Lord anymore! I can't believe I have given people and their opinions such power over me. I can't believe I've allowed other people to define me. I can't believe I've believed other people's opinions over God's Word!"

How about you? What things have crippled you? What things from the past are still present with you? What would cause you not to see God's plan for your life? In Ephesians 1:18 the apostle Paul prayed this profound prayer of revelation: "I pray that the *eyes of your heart* may be enlightened in order that you may know the hope to which he has called you" (emphasis added). *Wow!* Your heart not only has a brain, but it also has eyes—eyes that need to be enlightened so that you will be able to see the hope to which you were called. It's not enough for our natural eyes to be opened. The "eyes" of our hearts must be opened!

Paul then goes on to pray in verses 19–22 that we would know (in our hearts) "his incomparably great power for us who believe." (Can't we see now why the enemy wants to keep believers from believing?) He goes on to say, "That power is the same as the mighty strength he exerted when he raised Christ from the dead and seated him at his right hand in the heavenly realms, far above all rule and authority, power and dominion, and every name that is invoked, not only in the present age but also in the one to come. And God placed all things under his feet."

Wow. This makes so much sense. This shines the spotlight on why God's people have been so slow in understanding not only the hope that belongs to them but also the incomparable power that belongs to those of us who belong to Him. We must pray, "Open the eyes of my heart, Lord. I need to see You!" It's imperative that the eyes of our hearts see Him high and lifted up!

Let's Pray

Holy Spirit, please open the eyes of my heart so that I would truly gain understanding and a new depth of insight to know who You are and who I am in You. Clean my heart with Your Word, from all those negative opinions that I've allowed to define me. Cause me to allow Your Word to have the run of my house. I thank You that You chose me to succeed from the foundations of the earth. Thank You that I am truly able to love You because You loved me first. Thank You that I am already on the road to victory because of the power that lives in me. In Jesus's name, amen.

CHAPTER 3 – ASHES, ASHES

Imagine shopping from gourmet store to gourmet store, gathering luscious ingredients with only one expectation: to make your favorite person a scrumptious meal. *Yum!* You proceed to get out the cookbook and follow the recipe to a tee. You slice and dice and place all the ingredients gently into the pan, but there is a small issue—the pan is coated with leftover ashes from the last feast you prepared. At this point it doesn't matter how much time was spent on the shopping or if the ingredients were organic and the preparation was tedious. It wouldn't even matter if the recipe was one of Oprah's favorite things. The meal would be ruined—a total disaster, with yucky bits of burned ash meshed into every morsel.

The Book of Leviticus was heaven's sacred recipe book, filled with ways to cook up different types of worship meals for different seasons. There were different requirements, or "recipes," for each feast day or Day of Atonement or day of grief. It was sort of like a family's traditional recipe book. There were clearly different meals for different holiday feasts.

In my husband's family, on Christmas Eve there was never any meat. Meat on Christmas Eve would upset all the holiday festivities. No way! Fish was where it was at. The whole fish and nothing but the fish! Different types of seafood were plentiful. For example, there's shrimp prepared scampi style, cocktail style, and fried with bread crumbs. There's calamari, prepared in a salad or fried, with sauce or without. And there's always linguine with clam sauce, red or white. Someone also takes on the tedious job of making rice balls, spinach rolls, and zeppole with powdered sugar (*delicious!*). But there was *never* any red meat or poultry!

On Christmas Day, however, everything changed. Different recipes for different days, and you could never mix them. On Christmas Day Grandma prepared her once-a-year traditional meat sauce. This had to simmer on the stove a minimum of six hours. It included a variety of meats, which had to be placed into the massive pot at different intervals. The braciole, which is a piece of beef stuffed with cheese and parsley, and the pork spareribs went in first. They had to soften until they fell off the bone. Hours later in went the sausage and lastly the meatballs. This aromatic medley of meats cooked for hours in a huge pot of garlic, oil, onions, and tomato sauce seasoned to perfection.

You *could never* leave one of those meats out. In fact, you *would never* leave out one of those ingredients, because if you did, the family elders would put on their sackcloth and ashes and cry out at the top of their lungs, "Mama mia!" The heads of the family—the judges—wouldn't even consider it a meat sauce without each of those meats. And without the meat sauce it just wouldn't be Christmas.

But no matter how magnificent the Christmas feast turned out, everyone looked forward to Easter, which was right around the corner. No meatballs on Easter Sunday. That would be a sacrilege. It was leg of lamb. And there was a whole different code for the spread prepared after a funeral. There you had the typical antipasto platter. This included cold meats, sliced, with an array of different cheeses accompanying different types of bread—seeds or no seeds, semolina or white flour, hard crusted or soft. Different requirements for different occasions!

The traditional recipes for worship spoken of in the Book of Leviticus had to be followed perfectly, each according to the code of heaven. No shortcuts! Of course, we don't offer sin offerings any longer because Jesus died once and for all for our sins. We don't have fellowship offerings per se, because now we can have fellowship with the Lord anytime, all the time. But the one offering that has so much typology that still can be applied to our everyday life is the burnt (or consumed) offering. In Leviticus 6:8–13 we find a recipe for the priests to come before the Lord for no other reason than to have alone time with God. This offering was for pure worship and intimacy, and the recipe explained the proper way to come into His presence.

The burnt offering was a foreshadowing of Jesus Christ, the Lamb of God slain to make it possible for us to have fellowship or intimacy with God. Although the Lamb was slain, the burnt offering hasn't been done away with; it's just done in a different form. As believers in Jesus we are priests of the Lord (1 Pet. 2:5; Rev. 1:6; 5:10), and our lives are to be offered up as living sacrifices to God, holy and pleasing to Him (Rom. 12:1). So the sacrifice is now alive, and the death we as priests die is to our flesh and our will, which is absolutely a daily, ongoing thing.

The burnt offering was different from any other offering or priestly duty. Every other offering was made on behalf of the people—it was for others. For example, the priest offered the grain offering so the people could have fellowship with God. The sin offering symbolized atonement and was offered so the people could be accepted in the sight of God. But the consumed offering was for God and God alone, an offering the priest made on behalf of himself. The Bible says this particular offering was a sweet smelling aroma to God. The fragrance of this offering traveled all the way to the nostrils of God. Every time the priests offered the consumed offering, it was like they were sending an SOS signal to heaven, and what God saw was: *They love Me. They need Me!*

This offering is similar to our time of devotion in the mornings and evenings—an uninterrupted time set aside to pour out our hearts before God. How the Lord loves when we take time out of our busy schedules to just love Him and ask Him what He thinks we should do or not do. He loves when we honor Him by reading His Word, which is basically God's Heart in a nutshell on how to live life. When we spend time with God, it's just like sending Him a love telegram. We are saying, "I value Your opinion because Your thoughts are way higher than my thoughts!"

Realize this: everything else the priests did was for someone else. Yes, the priests had hectic schedules and important responsibilities, but what about their own souls? What about the condition of their hearts? I'm sure they had plenty of annoying people in their congregations who were hard to handle. I'm sure there was sin in the camp. I'm sure that spending time with God was a much-needed station break to allow their flesh to cool down and to get their spirit fired up!

Simply put, although they were priests, they weren't perfect. Although they were God's men, they weren't God! They were human beings, which means they were being human. They needed their own time with God because they had their own issues, burdens, and regrets. They were dealing with their own fears and failures. Knowing this, God instituted this offering because He wanted the priests to have a time when they could pour out their guts before Him—and according to the requirements of this offering, it seems that their guts were exactly what God required. He wanted them naked, spilled out, and raw—nothing hidden! Plus, this offering allowed God to spend time with them—His favorite thing to do!

Think about it. Are we any different? Most of what we do in life is for other people, and realistically we really can't keep on helping others unless we get alone in God's presence and spend time in His Word and in prayer. All of us, just like the priests, have our own issues, burdens, and sins. Thank God we don't have to find a lamb, slit its neck, take the insides out, wash the organs, cut off the head and legs, trim the fat, and then place it perfectly in the line of fire, wait for the ashes to die down, change our clothes to go and throw the ashes on the ash heap, come back to the camp, change back into our priestly garments, and start all over! Thank You, Jesus, we don't have to do that today!

But we do have to come naked and vulnerable before Him. We do need to take out our inward parts and allow Him to wash them. We do have to consecrate ourselves every day—our eyes, ears, mouths, and legs—so He can direct our paths. And we must place ourselves in the line of fire so God can consume us and our issues!

This is not by any means following the law instead of grace. This isn't some staunch, legalistic ritual. This is like following Grandma's recipe for meat sauce, a recipe that has already been tried and tested! Let's face it; if you want great meat sauce, or a life of great worship, you just can't leave it up to chance. No, you follow the recipe of the experts, and success is sure to follow!

So if I could encapsulate this way of life, it would basically be this: in order for there to be a public declaration, there must first be private communion, private conversation. How can we speak to others on behalf of God if we don't speak to God first! We might be able to wing it in the beginning with the leftover flavor from the ashes left in the pan, but ultimately all people will swallow is ashes! When God instituted this offering, He was basically saying, "Spend time with Me and put it out there! Get it out in the open! Air your dirty laundry before Me, and I will take it and wash it— every dirty piece of it. I will sort it out and make you spotless in the process!"

Let me add that the fire on this altar also was different. God Himself came down and ignited the fire (Lev. 9:24), but it was up to the priest to keep it burning as stated in Leviticus 6:12. The verse clearly says the fire *must* be kept burning. *It must not go out*—and *we* are the keepers of the fire. It must burn morning and evening. This was known as the morning sacrifice and the evening sacrifice (Exod. 29:39; Lev. 6:8–13). The fire had to be kept burning because an altar without fire doesn't please God. When Israel backslid, they kept many of their ceremonies, but in Scripture we no longer see them presenting the consumed offering. That's just like us. When the fire on the altar of our hearts grows cold, the first thing to go is intimacy, our private time with the Lord, but we continue on in our Christian duties, growing stale and losing our effectiveness. (See Matthew 5:13–16.)

Applying This to Our Lives Today

These were the requirements for the burnt offering described in Exodus 29 and Leviticus 1:

- They had to take a live lamb—no dead sacrifices.
- The lamb had to be unblemished.
- Its skin had to be peeled back.
- Its neck had to be slit.
- Its organs had to be taken out, and each one had to be thoroughly washed, every crack and every crevice.
- Its head had to be cut off.
- Its legs had to be cut off.
- The fat had to be trimmed.
- And every piece of the lamb had to be arranged in the line of fire on the altar, which was front and center.

Once the offering was consumed or accepted, the priests had to carry the ashes outside of the camp, and the priest himself had to place the ashes onto the ash heap. Knowing that the burnt or consumed offering is symbolic of giving our everyday lives in worship to God, let's see how this very complicated process applies to our lives.

Whatever we offer to God must be alive.

Dead sacrifices were not acceptable then, nor are they acceptable for us today. Romans 12:1 says we are living sacrifices, not dead ones. Don't you see? *We* are the New Testament offerings God wants to consume! So the life we offer to God must be vibrant, full of passion—and the fire *must not go out!*

You don't "turn on" Sunday and then put the lights out on Monday! Wherever we go and in whatever we do, we must produce life-giving fruit. This is what sets real Christianity apart from every other organized religion. (By the way, "organized religion" is the antithesis of what Christianity is supposed to be. It's more like organized chaos. The Holy Spirit comes to mess up our everyday lives so someone else's life can be straightened out!) Our spiritual life is not to be put into a box. It shouldn't be compartmentalized. Our attitude should never be, "This is God's time and this is mine." No way! It's *all* His!

We call Christianity a religion, but the Christian life really is not about the rules and regulations of a denomination. *It's about life.* Every morning and evening—life! Our lives are supposed to be sending up an SOS to God continually, a fragrant aroma. Everything we do and say is ultimately to say, "I love You. I need You. Thank You for saving me!"

To do this, our lives must be arranged "in the line of fire." My hairdresser told me that she knew the people who came from our church. It wasn't because they carried around big Bibles or because they preached a sermon every time they saw her. No, their lives were living epistles, and she was reading their behavior. Their kindness was evident. She said as soon as they sat in the chair she sensed life. She is now my friend and sister in Christ.

I also had another friend named Claire. She was a teenager who was friends with a girl who lived near us. When we both happened to be outside, Claire and I would have some light conversations. One day I came home and found Claire sitting on my front steps. I got out of my car and asked her if she was OK. She said that she would like to talk to me. I invited her inside. Her exact words were, "There's something different about you and your family. What is it?" I told her that it was Jesus. He makes all the difference in our lives. This young Irish Catholic girl received Christ, and in turn, many of her family members got saved.

Our sacrifice must be holy in appearance.

Our living sacrifices must be unblemished outwardly. This means we must conduct ourselves in a manner worthy of the gospel we represent. We are Christ's ambassadors; therefore, our conduct, behavior, and appearance should represent Him. God cares about our conduct with outsiders because God so loves the world, and He doesn't want our outward behavior to be inconsistent with the gospel message we are called to proclaim!

Allow me to give you a personal testimony. I moved into my house in 1978, and my husband planted a small pine tree, which through the years grew to at least sixty feet. We loved that tree. It shaded our small backyard. (We are New Yorkers, so our property is 45 feet by 95 feet.) The arms of the tree served as both a gigantic umbrella and a blanket of privacy. None of my neighbors could see inside my home because the tree blocked the view of my home for hundreds of feet. The arms also extended to my three neighbors' yards. It was a great tree.

One Friday evening as I was walking around the corner with one of my granddaughters to mail a letter, I saw my brand-new neighbor come out of his driveway. I introduced myself and pointed to my house. He said, "Oh, you are the one with the tree?" I said, "Yes, is my tree bothering you?" He went on to say, "Well, let's put it this way, your other neighbor and I are willing to chip in and help to pay to chop the tree down." *What?* My next-door neighbor, whom I have known forever, was talking about me and hated my tree? My new neighbor said the sap from the tree was making a real mess on his property. I totally understood, because it was making a real mess on mine too. I assured him that it was my tree and therefore it was my problem.

As we walked away, my granddaughter said defensively, "Nana, who does that man think he is? That's your tree, Nana, and it's none of his business!" I said, "No, the Bible tells us to live in peace with everyone as long as we have it in our power to do so." I went home and explained the situation to my husband, and he agreed that we needed to cut the tree down. The next day we called a tree service, and as it turned out, they just happened to be in our neighborhood and said they could come right over. I swallowed real hard and said OK. I certainly wasn't expecting such quick action to be taken. The serviceman then gave us a very affordable price and said he could take the tree down immediately. I swallowed hard again, but I knew this wasn't as much about the tree as it was about being obedient to God's Word.

As they were cutting the tree down, I was on my second floor looking out the window. I was crying over this tree that had become part of our family. The more they cut, the more of the neighborhood I saw—neighbors I hadn't seen in three decades. I felt like my house was like a girl without her dress on. It was pitiful. The tree made my backyard look majestic, but now it looked naked. I just kept saying, "Lord, I'm doing this for You!" But I didn't want to see the tree go. During the services on Sunday I was so heartbroken. On Monday I left with my assistant to preach at a women's conference in Texas, and while I was there, I kept taking pictures of trees that grew tall and did not shed. When the pastor's wife asked me what I was doing, I told her my tale of woe.

The conference was awesome, and the Lord really helped me to minister, so I temporarily forgot about my naked backyard. When I went back to my room after one of the sessions, I noticed that I had a voicemail on my cell phone. It was my daughter-in-law. She was crying and said, "Mom, New York City had a tornado, and all the trees have been pulled out of the cement at the roots. Our neighborhood was hit the hardest, a total disaster area." New York City just doesn't have tornadoes. I was astounded. Our gardener said that if we had not taken the down the tree, it would have crashed into our home, causing major damage. *Whew!* I thought, "God, I thought I was doing something for You, but You were really doing something for me!"

The story doesn't end there. One year later, while walking around the block to mail yet another letter, I saw my neighbor. I said, "Hi, remember me? I'm the one with the tree." He said, "Yes, I remember." I got to witness to him as I explained why I had taken the tree down. His wife came outside and said, "Now I know who you are. I've been looking out my window into your backyard, and I couldn't place your husband, but I knew I had seen him before." Then she said, "Now I know. I've been visiting your church the last few weeks!" *Wow!* Come on! By living as though I was representing Christ and not myself, I became a witness to my neighbors!

God is concerned about both our public life and our private life.

Before the priest could offer the sacrifice:

- The animal's neck had to be slit and the flesh peeled back. I believe this symbolizes transparency and vulnerability. We are to be laid bare before God. No pretenses. Everything in the light, nothing hidden.
- The inward parts had to be taken out—exposed and washed, every crack and every crevice. It's as Psalm 51:6 says: He desires truth in the inward parts.
- The head had to be cut off and laid on the altar. I believe this symbolizes us bringing our thought life before the Lord. The head also includes our eyes and ears, representing what we watch and what we give ear to, as well as our mouth, symbolizing what we speak about. We have to lay all of these things on the altar.
- When I got saved, I placed a note on my telephone. It was a reminder that the Holy Spirit was listening to my conversation, so I had better be careful what came out of my mouth. I had to

beware of gossip, slander, and making critical statements, which I had a propensity to do. I think I should still keep that note on every phone in my house and on my cell phone as a reminder to keep from saying anything that would displease the Lord.

- The legs had to be cut off and laid on the altar, which says to me that we must allow the Holy Spirit to control our steps.

- The heart had to be washed and placed on the altar, which of course symbolizes our emotions and attitudes. Our heart needs to be continually cleansed, every day, morning and evening.

- The fat had to be trimmed off and laid on the altar. The fat symbolizes all of our accomplishments. Yesterday's victories are great, but God wants to give us new victories today. He doesn't want us focusing on the past and missing the things He has for us in the future. I had a friend who studied Jewish history and the traditions of the priests. She told me that as the offering was being consumed, the priests would walk in front of the altar in the formation of the number eight. Of course, the number eight is symbolic of new beginnings. When the last ash fell to the ground, the priest would blow his trumpet and run from one side of the camp to the other, shouting, "It is finished! It is finished!" There was such excitement because when the ashes were gone, it meant that God accepted the sacrifice. Sin, failure, regrets—they all had gone up in smoke, no longer recognizable. It was now a new beginning! By faith they believed that they were made worthy and acceptable in the eyes of God.

The Ash Heap

As a last step, when the priest put down his trumpet, he had to change his garment so as not to soil it. He then had to put on a different set of clothes and immediately clean away *all the ashes on the altar* and carry them outside of the camp (Lev. 6:8–12). Then, once outside the camp, he had to throw them onto the *ash heap*. Yep, it was really called the ash heap—that was a real place.

In the midst of all of that fiery worship, God saw fit to have the priest take a break, change his clothes, and gather up the charred remains to get rid of every single ash. This was something the priest had to do himself. No one else could carry the ashes for him. He had to place his ashes on the ash heap himself. Doing this was almost like cleaning up a crime scene so there would be no evidence left that there was ever anything dead on that altar—it would look like it had always been a clean area to worship the Lord. When the priest came back into the camp, he was to change his clothes again, and on a clean altar was a fresh sacrifice.

Think about the typology or symbolism of the ash heap. The ash heap was a visible reminder that all the sins and situations of the day were given to God. The priests weren't allowed to take a break and eat a bowl of matzo ball soup or a brisket sandwich. There was no lying down on the job. Nope, the ashes had to be immediately removed from the altar of worship, because then and only then could they have the opportunity to start all over again with a brand-new time of worship. God knew that everyone needs a brand-new start.

For the priests this particular type of offering was done often, which simply tells me that everyone has ashes all the time. Life happens. Things happen each day that need to be burned up in God's presence and then forgotten so we can move forward. This step of removing the ashes was just as important as any step prior.

The priest was told to carry his own ashes to place them on the ash heap. No one else could do it for him—not a servant or even a close friend could carry the ashes out. The priest had to do it himself. He had to tangibly throw those ashes onto the ash heap and walk back in freedom. I bet as they were walking toward the ash heap, carrying their ashes, the priests would take the opportunity to rejoice and thank the Lord for accepting everything they offered to Him that day. Isn't that an incredible thought?

As mentioned earlier, when the priests returned to worship the Lord again, they had to change their clothes. New clothes represented new life. There would be neither stain nor smudge, not a hint of ash on the fresh garment. Brand-new robes for a brand new sacrifice! Yesterday's ashes had nothing to do with today's sacrifice. Every day was a fresh start. Leaving the ashes on the altar would be like rehashing the past. It wouldn't matter if the next sacrifice was unblemished and neatly laid on the altar as God instructed—the offering would be *unacceptable*! The integrity or the purity of the fire would be compromised. Ashes hinder the fire from burning brightly. Ashes weigh the fire down. Ashes cannot ascend in fire, so they hinder its brilliance. Ashes on the altar are an insult to the one receiving the offering. It would be like trying to cook a fresh meal for a king with yesterday's soot.

Well, that's how it is when we try to worship the King of kings with yesterday's regrets, failures, disappointments, confessed sin, and, yes, even our accomplishments. Instead of a vibrant altar life with fresh consecration front and center, we start to live a dark life, full of condemnation, fear, and secrecy. We end up trading the altar for a closed urn where the ashes of the dead are placed, the remains of something that has passed away. Think about where people place an urn. It's usually on a mantel—a glorified shelf that is front and center. It is given a place of prominence.

Every time you see the urn, you remember whose ashes are inside it. Make no mistake about it; *ashes have a voice!* It is next to impossible to have a new relationship with your late loved one glaring at you. Even though the person is dead and gone, we are still somehow connected to him, still tied—stuck. Well, when we hold on to our old ashes, we unintentionally *protect the ashes and neglect the fire!* The ashes become sacred and untouchable. We end up memorializing our past. We dress the ashes in a beautiful decorative jar, and people encounter nothing but death when they meet us. We become nothing more than *decorated religious jars*, stuck in our past.

Of course, I did a small study on urns by speaking to a funeral director. Allow me to give you some urn facts:

- **Urns are fireproof**—the fresh fire of God cannot penetrate.
- **Urns are waterproof**—the water of God's Word can't wash us.
- **Urns are airtight**—the breath of God cannot revive us.
- **Urns are heavy**—living in the past is a heavy weight to carry around.

The urn keeps the light out. It hides the glory and keeps the past intact! So it is virtually impossible to have a healthy, vibrant daily life of passionate worship with the heavy weight of the past on your chest. I know we absolutely understand this in theory, but the voices in our hearts constantly contradict the voice of the Holy Spirit, who constantly admonishes us, "Let it go!"

Don't you think it's about time we take an eighteen-inch walk to the ash heap and leave all our regrets and failures there? Isn't it time to open the vault of your heart where all of the secrets of your past are locked up, take the lid off, and allow the light of God's presence to shine deep down on the inside, and then allow His wonderful, loving voice to drown out the tired rhetoric of your past?

Romans 6:17 says, "Thanks be to God that, though you used to be slaves to sin, you have come to obey from your heart the pattern of teaching that has now claimed your allegiance." Notice the transaction from being a slave to sin to a slave to righteousness. No longer are we under the law, but under this new pattern of grace. Once this new allegiance occurs, accepting this covenant of grace becomes relational as opposed to just doctrinal. The change must take place *in the heart!* Herein lies the journey from our head to our heart.

Theologically the past is already dead. It has been crucified with Christ (Gal. 2:20), and its voice was silenced on Calvary more than two thousand years ago. So go ahead, give your past a proper burial, and start today fresh and new. Oh, believe me, we will always have ashes, but I pray that now we know where to place them.

No one is exempt from this. God told Samuel, His prophet, "How long will you mourn for Saul . . . ? Fill your horn with oil and be on your way" (1 Sam. 16:1). The Holy Spirit was gently prodding the prophet to let the past go and move forward. Had Samuel continued to mourn for Saul, he would have never anointed David. There's a David in our lives who will replace our Sauls. There are giants waiting to be taken down, and we are just eighteen inches from the victory.

What "Saul" might you be mourning over? Is it some relationship that didn't work out? Is it a ministry that may have failed? Maybe it's a dream that has died. Maybe it's a constant conversation with past failure and guilt that keeps you stuck in a rut. Maybe it's a tape recorder that plays over and over again words that have wounded you deeply and that you have mistaken for the voice of God, leaving you believing that is the way He feels about you. Because of that tape of lies, you can't have private time and communion with Him—you're too afraid of Him. When you read scriptures that say things like, "Sit still, my daughter" (Ruth 3:18, kjv), you are afraid to do so because, truth be told, you think God won't show up. So instead of feeling rejected, you decide to busy yourself with everything but having a quiet time with God.

We can't walk forward while looking backward! Give the past to the Lord, and ask Him to wash away all the sludge that keeps you from taking a giant leap forward so the cycle of the past can be broken once and for all! We are supposed to be living sacrifices, not dead embers. Isaiah 61:3 says God will give us beauty for ashes, a garment of praise *instead of* a garment of heaviness. Why don't you take off the heavy load right now and slip into something much more comfortable?

Let's Pray

Lord, I don't want to be a decorated religious jar. I don't want to live my life on the shelf. I want to be a living sacrifice, holy and pleasing to You (Rom. 12:1–2). I think today is as good a day as any to bust out of the joint of my past, open the lid of the urn, and make a break for it—a prison break, that is! There's absolutely no reason for me to remain a prisoner of war in a battle that's already been won for me. I understand in my heart that there has been a changing of the guards, so I choose today to remove the weighty urn that sits front and center on the mantel of my heart, and replace it with the fresh fire of worship so that I may burn brightly for Your glory! In Jesus's name, amen.

Maria Durso

CHAPTER 4 – KEEP THAT FIRE BURNING

Does it strike you as odd that God is always comparing Himself with fire? His eyes blaze like fire (Rev. 19:12). The Book of Hebrews tells us that our God is a consuming fire (Heb. 12:29). Jeremiah 20:9 says His Word is like a fire. He showed up in the fire with the three Hebrew boys (Dan. 3:25). He was as a pillar of fire to keep His people warm in the wilderness (Exod. 13:21). On Mount Sinai He shows up in the form of a burning bush (Exod. 3:2). He said He would baptize us with fire (Matt. 3:11; Luke 3:16). In Acts chapter 2 tongues of fire fell upon the heads of Jesus's disciples (v. 3). So I would venture to say that apart from the fires of hell, fire is a good thing. God wants His people on fire, burning hot for Him!

These are the two trademarks of every born-again believer: the Holy Spirit, which symbolizes power, and the fire, which symbolizes our passion to use the power. I was changed by His power. Because of the indwelling of the Holy Spirit, my life was transformed from the inside out. I was one way one day, and then after my experience with Christ I was totally different.

I told you in a previous chapter about some of what I went through as a child. When I was ten years old, my father came and took me out of that awful boarding school. He happened to show up one day unannounced and found me all marked up, with a black eye and welts on my body. He immediately took me home to live in Manhattan.

Although I had lived a very difficult life emotionally, I was still very innocent. My new neighborhood, however, was not. I was placed in a coed school. I had never been around boys before. The boys liked me because I was the new girl, so therefore the girls hated me. The girls chased me home every day after school. They were giants to me. I was four foot eleven, and they were like the Philistines in the Bible—tall and strong. Every day I would get into my apartment and shut the door behind me huffing and puffing. When I'd arrive, my dad would have his glass of scotch in hand, looking out the window and still crying for my mother. He would ask, "How's everything, Maria?" To which I would always respond, "Fine, Daddy. Just fine."

One day the "Philistines" caught me and ripped my shirt in front of everyone. I didn't know how to fight then. I say "then" because I had to quickly learn. As I held on to my blouse with my left hand, I went to punch the girl with my right hand. She was so much taller than I was. I closed my fist, but I forgot to tuck in my thumb. I swung upward as hard as I could, and with that swing my thumb snapped; it was broken. But I couldn't go home and tell my father that my thumb was broken. I didn't want to be a "bother." So my thumb had to heal on its own. Because it was never set right, there are certain movements that are still very painful for me even after so many years.

I liken that broken thumb to the things in our lives that haven't been set right. Some movement, some smell, some song will bring us back to the scene of the crime. When we give our lives to Christ, He takes those things that need to be reset and fixes them. Although it is painful, He has to break those areas of our lives in order to reset them.

After that fight my thumb wasn't the only thing that snapped. I went from being a docile child to a girl who was very rebellious. I thought that if my dad didn't care for me, then why should I care for him? I started to drink cheap wine at the age of eleven. I would get so drunk, I would lie in the gutter in Manhattan's famous meat packing district in the spilled blood of butchered animals. I was a little girl stoned out of her mind and feeling hopeless.

My drinking escalated to drugs, and by the time I was eighteen years old, I was shooting heroin. I overdosed three times. I was arrested and spent the night in jail, but the police captain allowed me to go home without pressing any charges. I was so out of control that I set an apartment on fire when I punctured an aerosol can because I was so stoned.

When I was twenty-three years old, I found my father dead in his New York City apartment. I was so addicted that before I called for help, I took his prescription drugs and liquor. My dad left me a ton of money, and of course I thought that was the answer to my desperate loneliness. I had designer everything—designer from head to toe and the best drugs available. I worked for Bergdorf Goodman and did the makeup of the rich and the famous. But none of those things were ever able to fill the deep chasm in my soul.

I ended up meeting the love of my life, and after we dated a while we decided to move in together. We went to Bloomingdale's and ordered gorgeous furniture to fill our new studio apartment. We decided to go on a vacation to Mexico, sort of like a honeymoon except without the marriage license. We boarded a flight with my complete set of designer luggage and three thousand dollars worth of cocaine. I had a Norma Kamali string bikini and more chains than Mr. T.

We planned on partying but in this Mexican paradise, the strangest thing happened to me. Instead of feeling fulfilled, I felt emptier as the days went on. One evening my boyfriend, Michael, went out for a walk on the beach. I decided to stay behind, because I had determined that I was going to have a conversation with God! In our luxurious room I started to talk to Him . . . OK, so I started to curse Him out. I started to scream at the top of my lungs, "What kind of God are You? What is this thing called life? I feel like a dog chasing her tail!" Then in the midst of my tirade I heard something deep within my heart. It said, "Maria." Imagine that! God knew my name, the name that wasn't on my birth certificate. His exact words were, "Give Me your life before it's too late!"

I knew it was God, but I didn't know His name was Jesus. That voice filled the void I'd always had. It was sort of like mercury that rises in a thermometer. Imagine this holy God coming and speaking to this very unholy woman! I immediately felt an instant conviction of sin. I knew my filthy mouth was wrong, my string bikini, the drinking and drugging, and sleeping with my boyfriend. It was the strangest thing. I felt instant conviction of sin, but I didn't feel condemned. As a matter of fact, I felt a great sense of hope and worth.

When my boyfriend came back into the room, I asked him, "When we return home, would you go to church with me?" He said, "Church? You need to smoke a joint. You need to get high." I said, "I don't need a joint. I need God in my life." There were five more days in our vacation, and it seemed like a century. Michael was planning on dumping me because I closed up shop, and I was planning on dumping him because he wasn't interested in finding the voice, whoever it was.

As we were leaving the resort, I was approached to stay on and work there as a hostess. I remember saying to Michael, "That's the devil. He doesn't want me to go home and go to church!" I don't know how I knew that, but I did. We went back home, and I had to call somebody to tell about my experience. Of course, I didn't know any Christians. My friends were all druggies, just like me. I decided to call a friend I'll call Barbara. I said, "I've got to talk to you." And she said, "No, I've got to talk to you." But she told me to hurry and go first, so I told her of my experience in the hotel room in Mexico. Then she said, "Praise the Lord!" I said, "*What?* Praise the Lord? What in the world does that mean?" I had never heard that expression before!

When I left a short ten days before, Barbara used many different expressions with God's name in them, but never in a positive sense. She explained that while we were away, some hippie preached the gospel to her and thirty of our friends. They accepted Christ and had a prayer meeting for me and Michael! Guess what night that was? You guessed it—it was the night that voice spoke to me all the way in Mexico. She took Michael and me to church the next night, although my boyfriend was not exactly a willing participant. During the service he made fun of the preacher. He had cocaine in his pocket and figured I would get this ridiculous notion out of my system and we could get on with our lives.

At the end of the sermon, the pastor said, "If you were to die tonight, would you know where you would spend eternity?" I went forward. I felt like I moved involuntarily out of my seat. I felt like a thousand angels came down and started to wash all the filth off of me. When I looked to my right, guess who was kneeling next to me, weeping? You guessed it—Michael.

The pastor came and anointed us with oil. He said we would be known as the foolish things that confound the wise. We went back to the apartment that night and separated the mattresses on the floor. We threw out all the drugs and drug paraphernalia, the ungodly music and magazines, and all of our immodest clothes. We gave God our whole lives, and He gave us back a whole new life. Not long after that, we got married on a rainy Monday in City Hall. No fanfare—we just wanted to be right with God. That was in 1975. God in His great mercy has given me the most precious husband, who leaves me love notes every morning. Michael and I also pastor the greatest church, in our opinion, working alongside the most radically saved people you will ever have the good fortune to meet. We have three sons—Adam, Jordan, and Chris—who are all in the ministry and doing absolutely *incredible* things for God. I have daughters-in-law whom I love like my very own daughters, and the icing on the cake is that we have eight absolutely amazingly precious grandchildren. That night in that little church God set us on fire, and by God's grace it has never gone out!

Although I was instantly delivered from drugs and immorality, it would take *decades* for that *same fire* to burn away all the seeds of negativity that had taken root in the deepest recesses of my heart. Foresters say that some fires are good. They clear away debris that oftentimes hinders new life from growing. I definitely believe God used the fires in my life to bring to the surface the toxins that remained unseen, which I will continue to discuss in future chapters.

Why Fire?

Why do you think God would use the symbol of fire throughout Scripture, as we discussed at the beginning of this chapter? Well, there are certain properties of fire that I believe God wants to be evident in our everyday lives. Let's take a look at them.

Fire illuminates—it lights our pathway.

It is so important to live in the light of God's presence so He can expose every dark trap the enemy might place before us. Also, vision is imparted in the fire. When we are looking at the one whose eyes are like fire, we will be able to receive revelation for our own lives as we are led and directed by the Holy Spirit. People on fire hear the still, small voice within saying, "This is the way, walk ye in it" (Isa. 30:21, kjv).

Fire melts.

Fire changes the property of even the most hardened surface. It changes our hardened hearts. Life naturally makes us hard. We are not naturally pliable, moldable, or even stretchable. We are naturally fearful, small

34

minded, stingy, and petty—at least that's what I am without the fire of God. When we soak in the boiling oil of God's presence that has been heated by the fire of God, He changes what and who we are.

Consider this: Paul was a tentmaker. The only way a tentmaker could get the most bang for his buck was to take the hard hide of an animal and boil it in hot oil. When he removed the hard hide from the oil, the hide was stretchable, and the tentmaker was able to do so much more with it. It covered much more territory with less effort. But without the hot oil, the tentmaker could have pulled and pulled all he wanted but to no avail. The hide simply had no give.

The hide of the animal is so much like our hearts. No matter how hard we try or grit our teeth, our hearts aren't going to change—unless we get in the line of fire, in the direct heat of God's presence. The fact of the matter is, those ancient tents had to be taken down and soaked in boiling oil on a regular basis because the elements of nature, like the rain or the sun beating down on them, caused shrinkage. They had to be reboiled, re-stretched, and remolded. Life happens to us, but while the heat of life shrinks our heart's capacity, the heat of the fire of God enlarges our capacity. Just a little soaking in God's presence makes all the difference in our world and in those whom our lives affect.

Fire sterilizes.

Things that live in the smoke can't live in the fire. Fire has a way of bringing out the hidden vipers, venomous attitudes, and malignant or treacherous people who might be killing any spiritual life inside of us. The hidden things can be deadly, as we see in the story in Acts 28. The apostle Paul gathered a pile of brushwood, and as he put it on the fire, a viper, driven out by the heat, fastened itself on his hand. Had Paul not placed the wood on the fire, that viper would have remained hidden. I believe the Holy Spirit uses the fiery circumstances in our lives to expose and deal with the things that remain hidden—things that we learn to live with but that can cause great harm. Fiery trials have a way of purifying us. I think about the three Hebrew boys in Daniel 3. In the midst of the fire the only thing that was burned off was the chains that had them bound. Not a hair on their heads was singed, nor did their clothes even remotely smell like fire. Most of all, they saw the One who was walking with them in the midst of the fire. When they finally passed through that fiery circumstance, that horrible ordeal, everyone saw the glow of God upon them.

Fire radiates—it sets the temperature in the room.

The temperature is always changed by the presence of fire. Fire heats the house! As a boiler room is the source of heat in our house and sets the temperature, so the Holy Spirit, being the chief source of heat in our lives, should heat every cold place we come in contact with. Let's use the boiler room as an example of "holy heat" in our houses of worship. No one ever buys a house because he likes the boiler room. No one ever says, "Wow! What a boiler room. Oh, man, I love that boiler room!" No, initially people buy a house because they love the aesthetics—the wood floors, the granite countertops, the stainless steel appliances, etc. But think about it: if the house is cold because the boiler room is cold, it wouldn't matter what color the walls are painted or what material the countertops are made of. All eyes would be on the boiler room. Although it is tucked away, it is probably the most essential room in the house.

Without the boiler set at the right degree, the water temperature would never reach a comfortable level, and the pipes would freeze. That's how it is when behind the scenes in our houses of worship the leadership isn't hot for God—not on fire, or lacking "holy heat"! I often say, "No fire, no desire!" The leaders' passionless state would produce passionless worship because their altar of prayer would be cold and lifeless. If people came into the church, they would never feel comfortable enough to let down their guard and relax, just as they would never take their coats off and relax in a cold house where the boiler was broken.

If a church were cold, the guests would certainly be looking to the leadership to find out why there is no heat in the house of God. Only the fire of God's presence carried by desperate, passionate people who radiate His love could cause the fire of God to burn in a room. That's the difference between people visiting a church and saying, "I felt God's presence," and people leaving a service saying, "That was very nice." We don't want nice meetings. We must meet with the living God, for only He can change people's lives.

A boiler requires three things to operate smoothly. First, it requires clear pipes so clean water can flow through them. In much the same way, the pipes of our heart must remain clean so the water of God's Word can flow through. Second, a boiler must run without issues. It needs fresh supplies of oil on a regular basis. As the oil is used up, it must be replenished. So in our lives we must have fresh supplies of the oil of the Holy Spirit being delivered to us on a regular basis. The anointing must be replenished.

Last but not least, the boiler must have a constant flame burning.

The pilot light must always be on. Without the tiny flame there would be no hot water in the house. The oil would not be heated and the house would remain cold. Imagine that: the water that symbolizes God's Word and the oil that represents His anointing both need the tiny flame, because it is responsible for heating the gigantic boiler! Let's keep the flame of our hearts burning constantly. Don't ignore it! Although it seems insignificant, without it all the rest will remain cold. Remember, the fire on the altar must not go out! It must burn morning and evening.

Fire is contagious—it burns everything in its pathway.

Fire is not particular. It doesn't say, "I'll burn down the couch but not the table." Of course not! It burns everything in its way. When fire touches something, there is no mistaking it. There is an indistinguishable smell after a fire. God has created us to be spiritually combustible, spiritual pyromaniacs—human torches somehow affecting everyone in our path. We are to be a sweet smelling aroma to God.

People on fire leave a distinctive scent behind. When you are truly on fire, you don't hide behind religious walls. You are not particular about the type of person you reach out to—the color of their skin or their economic background. When you are on fire, you are not intimidated by external matters. Without realizing it, you touch everything around you with your presence in some way, shape, or form.

Remember this: God doesn't only judge faithfulness, but He also judges temperature! In the Book of Revelation there were two churches with temperature problems. One was the Laodicean church. The members were neither hot nor cold but lukewarm (Rev. 3:14–22). The other was the Ephesian church (Rev. 2:1–7). They left their first love; they lost their passion. Brothers and sisters, we need to be "packin' holy heat"—no concealed weapons.

Hot For God

Another thing that must remain "hot for God" is our gifts. Paul told Timothy in 2 Timothy 1:6–7 to fan into flame the gift of God within him. The implication is that the gift inside can remain dormant if we don't fan the flame. Paul is basically telling his son in the faith, "You'd better bring that gift to the boiling point. You seem to have lost sight of the gift of God that is already inside you. Listen, Timothy, God hasn't given you a spirit of fear. Don't be a coward. Don't allow fear to smother the flame that will ignite the gift!"

The solution to every difficult situation in this world, then and now, is the gift of God in us in one form or another. And guess what? The gift of God is within every single believer! Every believer has the gift the Holy Spirit deposited inside of them, and through them the Holy Spirit will display particular gifts according to the way God has made them! The church is the answer to the world's problems—it's not the other way around. He has anointed *us*!

- The answer to paganism is the gift of evangelism.
- The answer to wrong doctrine is the gift to rightly divide the

Word of truth.

- The answer to needs is the gift of giving.
- The answer to discouragement is the gift of encouragement.
- The answer to condemnation is the gift of mercy.
- The answer to unbelief is the gift of faith.
- The answer to disorganization is the gift of administration.
- The answer to wrong motives is the gift of discernment.
- The answer to loneliness is the gift of hospitality.
- The answer to sickness is the gift of healing.
- The answer to confusion is the gift of wisdom.

Come on, let's fan into flame every gift that God has given to us. Let's not allow anything to put our fire out. No unconfessed sin. No hurt or disappointment. No religious people who think they are supposed to be fire extinguishers instead of spiritual pyromaniacs. Don't allow anything to get you to simmer down. Don't listen to any lie of the enemy that reminds you of your past and discourages you from fulfilling your future. And most importantly, don't neglect your fire, allowing devotion to be turned into duty! It has been said that it's the nature of the fire to automatically go out. Don't let that happen to you. Tend to the fire in your heart and allow the Holy Spirit to continually breathe on you so that people say, "Wow, she's hot," or, "Wow, he's hot"—and may they mean we are burning hot for God! Come on, it's time for a *brain wash*!

Let's Pray

Lord, set us on fire. Consume us through and through. Set every gift that You have placed in us, gifts that may be lying dormant, to the boiling point. Let us be a bright light set ablaze affecting this dark world. In Jesus's name, amen.

CHAPTER 5 – DOES *FAVOR* MEAN *FAVORITE?*

Most of us, for whatever reason, have weird stereotypes or distorted views about who God really is, whom He could possibly use, how He acts or reacts, and what certain concepts in His Word really mean. Because of these misconceptions, our Christian lives are relatively joyless, and we get bent out of shape trying to accept the very things that are supposed to be blessings. I would like to put a small dent into some of those distortions and take a load off our minds.

Let me start with this example. Between the Old Testament and the New Testament there is a span of four hundred years. The Book of Malachi doesn't exactly end on a high note. Man is estranged from God, many priests are corrupt, and the Lord says a "day of fire" is coming. Then for hundreds of years there is deafening silence. Man heard nothing from God. There was no prophet to speak on His behalf.

So here comes the New Testament, and now God finally speaks. What do you think He would say? What would His tone be? Would He be disgusted and issue a scathing rebuke? Would He pull out a rap sheet listing all the offenses committed or go on a tirade about how disappointed He is with mankind? And after all those years, whom do you think He would speak to?

Just when we think we have God all figured out, He defies human logic. When He finally spoke again after four hundred years, He sent a greeting! If that doesn't shatter every stereotype we have of God, consider this: not only does He send a greeting, but also He sends it to a "nobody," according to the who's who of religious society. That nobody lived in a no-name town—and to top it all off, that nobody was a *she*!

Let's absorb this for a moment. God came to a teenage girl, *not* a Pharisee, an expert in the Scriptures. He came to a no-name town, *not* Jerusalem, where the religious elite lived, and ended four hundred years of hopelessness with a divine visitation in the form of a greeting!

Wow! Wow! Woohoo! Did you catch that? The Bible records that an angel visited this young teenager named Mary and told her that not only was she highly favored but also that the Lord was with her! Can you imagine? If an angel swooped into your room and told you that you were not just *favored* but *highly favored* and chosen by God to be the mother of the Messiah, what would you think those words meant? What would go through your mind? How would you react?

If I was a young teen engaged to be married to a carpenter and I was told that I was *highly favored*, my immediate reaction would be to call my fiancé. Let's think about what Mary's conversation with Joseph might have been like in the 2014 version of the birth announcement: *[Ring, ring, ring.] Hurry up, Joe, pick up. Hello, Joseph. It's me, Mary. Listen, according to the angel that swooped into my house . . . Yes, Joe, an angel came right into the room. I saw him with my own two eyes . . . Listen, he said that I was highly favored. So listen up, this is what I'm thinking. Let's cancel the backyard wedding. I'm booking the wedding at the Jerusalem Hilton. Oh, and by the way, we are going to have a baby! Don't ask. I'll explain later. I'll call the office of Dr. Abraham; he's the chief obstetrician at Beth Israel Hospital . . . Census? What census? Eighty miles? On a donkey? Donkey? We don't need no donkey, Joseph. No, just tie that beast back up. I'm sure the angel will be sending a chariot with a driver for us. We are going in style, first class all the way! You've got to start thinking big, Joe.*

In this day and age somehow the word *favored* has gotten convoluted even within the body of Christ, and it has caused a separation. We think there are spiritual "haves" and "have-nots." The "haves" have it made in the shade. They have sunshine on a cloudy day, and when it's cold outside, they've got the month of May. They drive fancy cars, and have stainless steel appliances and perfect children. They never struggle, they are never sick, they are a size zero, and their husbands go to Tiffany's to buy them expensive jewelry because they were promoted to CEO of their companies. But that is not even close to the biblical meaning of *favor*. I think that we might need a brain wash!

Let's see Mary's real reaction when she was told that she was highly favored:

> Mary was greatly troubled at his words and wondered what kind
> of greeting this might be.
>
> —Luke 1:29

In other words, Mary was skeptical, just as we would be. She must have been thinking, "Me? Highly favored?" The word translated "troubled" in Luke 1:29 is such a strong and intensive verb, it is not used anywhere else in Scripture. It has the connotation of being greatly agitated or greatly upset. Mary was in turmoil. She couldn't process the salutation. She couldn't receive the affirmation. I'm sure Mary thought just as we would think: Isn't favor for some elite group? Isn't favor for people with perfect lives? The greeting didn't match up with her surroundings or her circumstances. She must have wondered, "Could anything good come from me? Could anything good come from Nazareth?" That's what people often said about the town—could anything good come from Nazareth? It was a no-name, ghetto, poor town, not like Jerusalem, where the religious elite lived.

So here we clearly see that favor has absolutely nothing to do with location. Mary was pledged to be married to a no-name carpenter. To put it in modern terms, Joseph was a blue-collar worker. So we also see that favor has nothing to do with vocation!

The angel didn't say, "Greetings, Mary. You are highly favored because you're perfect, you never miss the Sabbath, your skirts are always the perfect length, you don't paint your lips, and you always study the Scriptures." If only the angel had said something like that and given her a reason she'd been called highly favored just to take the mystery out of it so Mary could keep on doing whatever she was doing and continue to be favored!

Many times we think favor has something to do with our performance. But maybe—just maybe—she was favored because God the Father knew beforehand that she would be the perfect mom for the Messiah. Maybe that was it—maybe God knew that His Son, Jesus, would be safe in the arms of Mary. That makes perfect sense to me. *Yes!*

But in Luke 2, just one chapter later, Mary has a small mishap. Mary loses Jesus for three days in crowded Jerusalem. Oops! It even took her a whole day to realize that He wasn't among them. This is like the Middle Eastern version of the movie *Home Alone*. Jesus is twelve years old roaming the streets alone in a busy city, fending for Himself. This sounds like a case for Child Protective Services and CNN to investigate. To top it off, when Mary finally finds Him, she says, "Son, why have you treated us like this?" (v. 48). Can you believe it? Mary blames the kid!

Jesus answered, "'Did you not know that I must be about My Father's business?' But they did not understand the statement which He spoke to them" (Luke 2:49–50, nkjv). Really, Mary, are you kidding me? After all, if anyone knew who the "real Father" was, it was surely Mary. She doesn't seem to have the sharpest spiritual antenna. So here we see that favor has nothing to do with being the sharpest Christian in the pew.

Just to be clear, God really does use imperfect and unlikely people. He chose Abraham to father a nation, yet because Abraham initially didn't trust God in his heart, he fathered a child outside of God's perfect will. Moses messed up the whole deliverance program by killing an Egyptian because hatred ruled in his heart, setting the whole program back forty years. David, the one after God's own heart, committed adultery because lust ruled for a short season, and then he had the husband killed to cover his tracks because fear ruled in his heart. Let's not even bring up what was going on in Samson's heart! Yet God calls these men heroes of the faith—*favored*, if you will! They surely didn't "deserve" to be in the Hall of Faith in Hebrews 11. They didn't "deserve" to have their footprints on heaven's walk of faith. Yet they are there.

In yet another incident, in Matthew 12:46–50, Jesus is speaking to the multitudes. Let's picture this. Jesus is in the midst of a giant crusade. The Bible says His mother and brothers were standing outside, behind the scenes, waiting to speak with Him. What could be so important—more important than what He was doing? What could she and His half-siblings possibly want? Did they want to know if Jesus was going to be late for dinner? Did Mary want to ask Him why He didn't clean up His room? I kind of get the impression that Mary was a normal mom with the same controlling issues that we all have.

Jesus, being pulled away from His Father's business, responds by saying, "Who is my mother, and who are my brothers? . . . Whoever does the will of my Father in heaven is my brother and sister and mother" (Matt. 12:48, 50). *Wow!* That's pretty straight to the point. So here we see that favor doesn't mean we have Jesus wrapped around our finger or that He will always give us what we want.

We also know from Scripture that there was strife in Mary's home, a lot of sibling rivalry. The siblings were a bit cantankerous to Jesus. They would say things like, "If You really want to be famous, You should go into the big towns so You could make a name for Yourself!" (See Mark 6:4; John 7:1–5.) They were jealous and rude! When we think about Jesus and the home He grew up in, we oftentimes think that it was Jesus, Mary, and Joseph, and that's it. We picture Jesus multiplying the groceries, His sandals never touching the floor as He floats around the house. But that's not even close to the truth! Just imagine any of your siblings claiming that he or she is God. How would you react? So favor also doesn't mean we will have the most perfect home environment or do everything perfectly as parents, spouses, friends, etc.

Favored, Yet Going Through Trials

According to human standards, Mary's life was anything but perfect. If *favor* means everything is handed to us on a silver platter, then the angel lied to Mary. She was nearly dumped by Joseph until an angel intervened and spoke to Joseph in a dream. She was sent far away to the hill country to her cousin Elizabeth's house to hide her growing belly. (I wonder if that started the trend of parents sending their unwed pregnant daughters far away because they were ashamed.) She also had to ride eighty miles on a donkey a week before her due date. *Ouch!* That couldn't have been fun. And Luke 2:6 says "while they were there" (Where's "there"? Eighty miles from her loved ones!) she goes into labor.

There was no room at the Bethlehem Comfort Inn, and there were no midwives, no boiling pot of water, and no sterile rags. There was nothing but a carpenter—a fiancé who was there to help deliver a baby who wasn't even his—and hay soaked in urine and the stench of manure, which is so symbolic of our condition when Jesus is born in the stable of our hearts. The baby was born in subpar accommodations. The baby of "highly favored" Mary, the "King of kings," was born in a stinking stable. Jesus's entourage were barn animals! And to add insult to injury, Jesus isn't on the earth for five minutes before there's a war between the two kingdoms. There's immediate chaos because Herod the king wants to kill the King of kings.

Mary barely gets a chance to catch her breath before there is a threat on the child's life. Mary and Joseph have to find refuge in Egypt, not exactly a welcome place for a "good, respectable Jew." No grandma and grandpa to coddle and dote on Jesus. No baby or wedding shower. No family to help Mary out during this season of "favored" Mary's life.

But get ready, there's a change a comin'. Joseph and Mary must have been ready for some much-needed encouragement. Joe and Mary get back to the family. They go to the temple to dedicate their baby on the eighth day in accordance to the law requiring every firstborn male to be consecrated to the Lord. Perhaps there was a small dinner prepared for them after this joyous occasion. So as the courageous couple stands holding in their arms the hope of the world, whose care was placed upon their shoulders, a voice arises within the room and a word of prophecy is given. Finally, good news—a word of encouragement and affirmation to the faithful couple.

A public acknowledgment goes a long way, doesn't it? We can go through just about anything as long as we know God is pleased with us. It's a bonus when He confirms His pleasure to everyone we know. But the word wasn't anything like what Mary and Joseph were expecting. The voice cried out and spoke directly to "highly favored" Mary: "This Child is destined to cause the fall and rising of many in Israel and to be a sign which will be spoken against, so that the thoughts of many hearts may be revealed" (Luke 2:34–35, mev). OK, so far so good. But then the prophet Simeon drops a bomb on "highly favored" Mary: "*And a sword will pierce through your own soul also*" (v. 35, mev, emphasis added). Notice it doesn't say a sword shall pierce *your mind.* No, it says *your heart.*

Hasn't Mary's heart been pierced already? And isn't this a contradiction? Doesn't the Bible clearly state that she is blessed among women? If that is in fact true, and we know it is, the lesson we can learn is that we should never judge who is blessed and who is not by outward circumstances! Don't ever judge who is blessed and who is not by the type of car they drive or by the amount of money they have in the bank. The neighborhood you live in doesn't define whether you are blessed or not, nor does the size of the rock you wear on your finger. The obvious point is this: "blessed" people also go through major struggles that cause their hearts to be pierced or ripped to shreds.

Major bitterness could have set in Mary's heart after hearing that a sword, a bitter cup, a trial was coming that would pierce her *heart.* She had experienced a lot of disappointment since she said yes to God's will. And now these painful words were being spoken through the mouth of a prophet?

Wow! The state of Mary's heart was in jeopardy. Her heart was going to be attacked. Her baby was going to be misunderstood and rejected. A mother always feels the pain firsthand.

Everything hinges on the condition of the heart, as we will see again and again throughout this book. Oh, how Mary needed to protect her heart. As a woman thinks in her heart, so is she! Bitterness of heart will make the weight of a trial too heavy to bear. But Mary didn't become bitter. The Bible tells us in Luke 2:51 that Mary *treasured these things in her heart!* And because of the condition of Mary's heart, Jesus grew in wisdom and stature, and in favor with God and with man (v. 52).

Blessed Are The Pure In Heart

Because Mary was able to keep her heart clean, her pure heart served as a treasure chest that enabled her to see God in every circumstance. Matthew 5:8 says, "Blessed are the pure in heart, for they shall see God" (mev). Mary understood what the term *blessed* really meant, so there was *no room* in any part of her heart for the enemy or any divisive, discouraging thought to rest its evil head.

Let's think about this. According to the Bible's description, "favored people" just might experience closed doors, humiliations, inconveniences, and painful trials that will pierce their hearts. *Wow!* Now, because we can't compute what it means to be "favored"—just like Mary, who was greatly troubled when the angel told her she was highly favored—we go on an emotional roller coaster. One day we think God is angry at us, and the next day if we get a good parking spot we are whistling because we *feel* favored! All those feelings do is leave us schizophrenic, stressed out, straining, sour-faced struggling sistahs, sons, or saints!

I believe American Christianity has done a great disservice to us. When we bring our Western ideas to the text, we sadly misinterpret what God's favor really is. This magnificent, glorious truth has taken a backseat because in many ways it has been diluted and sabotaged by the thinking that if we are favored, then we should live an extravagant lifestyle like the rich and the famous.

As I was pondering how to understand favor in a way that was according to sound doctrine and in keeping with the events that happened to the first person who was told she was favored, the Holy Spirit woke me up one night and directed me to the Book of Ephesians. As I opened the Word, it became clear to me that what I thought "favor" was wasn't anything remotely close to the biblical definition. True, biblical favor has absolutely nothing to do with me or my lifestyle. So what exactly is the biblical meaning of *favor*, and was this royal treatment only for Mary?

The word translated *favor* in Luke 1:28 is used in only one other place in Scripture—in Ephesians 1:6: "Now all praise to God for his wonderful kindness to us and his favor that he has poured out upon us because we belong to his dearly loved Son" (tlb). The word *favor* in this context means freely accepted. So here we see "favor" is not "because"; it's "just because." We can interchange the word *favor* with the word *accepted* or *chosen*: "To the praise and glory of His grace, we *know* that He has [*chosen* or *accepted*] us in Christ" (emphasis added).

Favor is simply the undeserved, unearned, unmerited grace of God giving us what we never could have earned ourselves—not even on our best day; not even if we helped a little old lady or a blind man without a seeing-eye dog cross the street; not even if we were stuck in traffic for hours, late for the most important appointment of our life, yet we allowed a semitruck to cut in front of us, keeping our salvation intact! I once heard a preacher say, "He 'be-graced' us with His grace." Grace allows the one who was unacceptable to become acceptable in His presence "just because" of divine intervention—period!

Grace is putting us in the will before we were in the family. Before the foundations of the world God knew us and chose us anyway. He accepted us—actually picked us out as His own! When we didn't know Him, He knew us. You and I were on heaven's "most wanted" list. When we didn't want Him, He wanted us— the One who knows us the best loves us the most! We don't know why He loves us. There's no *because*—it's *just because*! When I was sinning, He saw a saint. Before we were clean, He saw us as spotless. When we stunk to high heaven, He smelled a sweet aroma. Before we ever uttered praise, He saw worshippers. Prior to my life beginning, God made a decision to love me through the thick and the thin; through the good, the bad, and the ugly! In Him we have forgiveness of sins, from the womb to the tomb. *Wow!* Now that's favor!

Because of this favor we have actually been placed inside of Christ. He covers us. He overshadows us just as the Holy Spirit overshadowed Mary! That certainly doesn't mean my life will be perfect, but it does mean that He who began this good work in me will complete it in me (Phil. 1:6)! He will work out all the kinks as we surrender our lives to Him. But first and foremost, we must *accept* being *accepted*.

The "Hail Mary Sin-Drome"

We are greatly troubled when it comes to accepting favor because we suffer from the "Hail Mary Sin-Drome." We focus on the word *virgin*—and there the comparisons begin. We are not like her, we are not special as she was, and we are not pure like her, so we conclude that we are not someone the Holy Spirit would ever want to fill. We think, therefore, that we are not favored. This is what happened to me. I saw the infilling of the Holy Spirit as the reward for reaching an unattainable goal.

I believe the fact that God used a virgin shows us that there is no other way to become filled with the life of God except by the overshadowing of the Holy Spirit. That which was *in her* was not *from her*—it was divine, unexplainable, and unattainable. Could it be that a "virgin womb" was just a prototype of a clean slate—an empty space, a place so barren that unless someone divine comes and fills it, it shall remain as it is? All the trying in the world can't fill it, and like Mary, the only way we can do anything for God is by the overshadowing of the Holy Spirit!

So could it be that Mary's response to favor is the only appropriate response: "May it be unto me according to your word" (Luke 1:38, mev)? In other words, I don't understand it, I know I definitely don't deserve it, *but* let it be done unto me as You say!

After Mary responded as she did, the Bible says then she began to worship. Worship is simply the response that comes from being accepted. My friends David and Nicole Binion, truly two of the greatest worship leaders and worshippers of our time, teach that real worship is simply love responding to love. The depth of our worship comes only from knowing the depths of how much we are loved!

We must accept being accepted. We must accept that we too are highly favored just because! If we don't accept this basic, fundamental truth, the enemy will leave us spiritually impoverished and bankrupt. We will be like spiritual orphans. The more we realize that we are accepted by God "just because," the more we will walk in victory no matter what challenges we might face. The hymn writer Frances J. Roberts wrote, "I have loved you simply because I have loved you, and what other reason do I need?"[1]

We need a spiritual DNC, a "deep-needed cleaning"—a brain wash! We need a washing of the brain of a heart that has been clogged by wrong thinking.

Come on, let's get what we know in our heads eighteen inches down into our hearts. Let's ask the Lord to help us remove all those distortions, stereotypes, false beliefs, legalistic attitudes, and every accusation that tells us we are not good enough. We are just eighteen inches away from the peace of mind that comes with knowing we are accepted!

Let's Pray

Lord, Your Word clearly instructs us to trust in the Lord with all our hearts, so I will do as it says. I'm not going to put my trust in my circumstances, past or present, nor go by what I see. Instead I am going to put all my trust in You, and You will make every crooked path straight as I acknowledge You and Your Word in all my ways for all of my days! In Jesus's name, amen.

Maria Durso

CHAPTER 6 – ABOVE ALL ELSE?

I'm a clean freak—an OCD, fanatical lunatic when it comes to cleanliness. It's something I picked up in the boarding school during my most impressionable years. I really thought the phrase "cleanliness is next to godliness" was in the Bible, and when I found out that it wasn't, I thought perhaps God or the one who wrote what was dictated made a small mistake. To me, there is no better feeling than knowing everything is clean. I can't stand clutter. Knowing everything is in order allows me to think straight. And there is nothing like the *smell* of clean. When I buy candles, I don't buy fruity or flowery fragrances. I buy candles that smell like clean laundry. The smell of freshly ironed cotton—I love it! *Hmmm.* Breathe in, breathe out!

I will come home late at night from a conference, where I might have spoken four to six times, and unpack, do *all* my laundry and anyone else's that hasn't been done, iron, and put it *all* away even if it's 3:00 a.m. I can have a hundred people crammed into my medium-sized home and feed them all, and I still will have the house spotless before I go to bed. I know what you are thinking by now: "Wow, she's nuts! She must be really hard to live with." It's not as bad as it seems. I just *love* to clean. I could be bone-tired from being in multiple services over the weekend and come home and mop for relaxation! I really like a clean house.

One morning a woman came to my house crying hysterically.

She had taken her twins to school and came home to find that her husband had taken all his things and moved out. Before I go on with the story, let me just say that I had been a Christian only a short amount of time and was not—I repeat—I *was not* in the ministry! The woman was crying as she sat at my *glass* kitchen table. She would wipe her face, blow her nose, and then press her fingers down on the table, making fingerprints. I subtly got a bottle of glass cleaner, and every time she would lift her hands to wipe away yet another tear, I would spritz a little cleaner and quickly wipe the table. This went on for probably two hours or so, but who's counting? Finally, as I went to gently clean away the smudges and residue left on the table by her tears for the thousandth time, she jumped up and said, "If you clean that table one more time . . . !" I can't repeat the rest.

As much as I love having a clean home, there is something that is so much more important. We need clean hearts because our hearts are the Holy Spirit's home, and the Holy Spirit deserves to live in a clean house. He deserves to live in a residence where His voice can be easily heard and His breath can be felt without any obstructions. Bottom line: God wants His people clean—squeaky clean. The one chore you have been given as a child of God is to keep your heart a dirt-free zone!

Jesus is not only the King of kings, but He is also the King of clean. I say this with all reverence and respect, but He is the original Mr. Clean. God doesn't like dirt. That's why He sent His one and only Son to clean up the mess we have made of things. If there were rugs in heaven, they would have perfect vacuum lines. If there were beds, there would be no dust balls underneath. Heaven is spotless. Jesus is the spotless Lamb. He is going to present His church without spot or wrinkle. He washed all our sins away.

The Word of God washes us daily. If husbands really want a clean home, they ought to wash their wives with the water of the Word. Jesus washed the disciples' feet. On the Mount of Transfiguration, Jesus' clothes turned brilliantly white—whiter than the garments in a Clorox bleach commercial. At the tomb His followers found Jesus' clothes neatly folded. He cleansed the temple of the money changers. He told the lepers to go and wash. Revelation 22:14 says those who have washed their robes in the blood of the Lamb have the right to enter heaven. In Matthew 23:25 Jesus basically told the Pharisees, "You clean the outside of the cup and dish, but inside they are full of greed and self indulgence." Ouch! Jesus is all about the inside. The Holy Spirit told Samuel, "Man looks at the outward appearance, but the Lord looks at the heart" (1 Sam. 16:7, nas). David wrote in Psalm 24:3–4, "Who may ascend the hill of the Lord? . . . He who has clean hands and a pure heart" (mev).

Oftentimes our standard of clean and God's standard of clean are very different. Sometimes the little things we learn to live with are totally unacceptable as far as God is concerned. But often we don't realize it until we come face-to-face with the light of God's Word. The Bible tells us that the entrance of His Word brings light (Ps. 119:130). Once we have an encounter with the truth, then what was acceptable before is acceptable no more!

I had a life-changing experience quite a while ago. A woman I know very well and whom I have known for a very long time asked to meet with me. She wanted to tell me about the brand-new work the Holy Spirit had done in her heart. She said for years she had a buildup, an accumulation of all this dirt in her heart against others, which led to depression and isolation. She said God cornered her and started to deal with her issue by issue. As she confronted and repented of each issue, she felt lighter and brighter. She said, "Maria, I don't ever want to go back to that place!" As she said those words, I was so convicted. I knew the Holy Spirit was dealing with me. I felt this holy jealousy stirring inside of me. I thought, "She's clean and I'm not." As a matter of fact, I had a degree in "offense-ology"!

I'd left a dust ball in the corner of my heart, and I needed to go after it as though it were an enemy invading my home. I wasn't being as meticulous with my heart as I was with my house. I wasn't living according to code, or according to God's Word. The Holy Spirit challenged me to clean my own heart. I woke up the next morning to a deep cry within my being, "A clean heart at all costs!" The Holy Spirit was challenging me, saying, "I don't want you to be a 'church woman.' I want you to be God's woman! I don't want you to be a woman who teaches the Word. I want you to be a woman who does what the Word says to do." The Word of God can't thrive in a dirty heart, but thank God we have His Word to clean up all the junk we have allowed to accumulate.

I've since learned that much more important than having a clean home is having a clean heart. There's nothing like it. What I'm about to share with you is not just something clever to read about and move on. It's a lifestyle. It's time for a brain wash!

Solomon, the wisest of all men, could have chosen anything as the most important thing in life. But inspired by the Holy Spirit, he penned the words in Proverbs 4:23: "Above all else, guard your heart, for *everything* you do flows from it" (emphasis added). *Above all else*, make this your number one priority: guard your own heart, for out of it flows *all* the issues of life.

The Message puts it this way: "Keep vigilant watch over your heart; that's where life starts." In other words, Solomon is saying if you get it wrong here, you will get it wrong everywhere. That's how vital a role our hearts play. Think about it this way: just as the earth spins on its axis, our hearts are the axis upon which everything in our lives spins. It's the true center from which all the shock waves radiate. The heart is where all the action is!

Everything is filtered through the lens of the heart. It's the source of our perceptions and understanding; therefore, it stands to reason that the heart calls the shots in our decision making. It's at the core of our being. Every experience passes through the heart. Every interaction is registered in the heart. The heart is involved in every facet of our lives. It's the entry point for good or bad. It's the seat of our emotions. That's why the Word of God urges us to aggressively guard our hearts. We are to give proper oversight to our hearts because they are our domain. The heart is a city, a metropolis, a universe within itself. Wars are fought on the bloody battlefield of the heart, and victory or defeat is determined in the heart.

Let's look at what the Scriptures have to say about the heart:

- Matthew 15:19 says out of the heart come evil thoughts, murder, sexual immorality, adultery, slander, and false testimony. So sin is conceived in the heart. The brain in the heart conjures up these destructive behaviors.
- Proverbs 12:25 says, "Anxiety in the heart causes depression." Fearful thoughts stored in the heart cause the heart to be weighed down or to sink.
- Jeremiah 17:9 tells us, "The heart is more deceitful than all things and desperately wicked; who can understand it?" (mev). *Wow!* You

can't possibly understand your own heart and its motives.

- Matthew 12:34 says, "Out of the abundance of the heart the mouth speaks" (nkjv). The heart has a 75 voice. Our lips are just parroting what our hearts are thinking.
- Psalm 14:1 says, "The fool has said in his heart, 'There is no God'" (mev). Atheism is a heart problem.
- Psalm 34:18 tells us that the heart can be broken. Thank God He binds up our broken hearts.
- First John 3:20 informs us that our hearts can feel condemned at times. But on the positive side, the heart has the capability of being pure. Matthew 5:8 says, "Blessed are the pure in heart, for they shall see God" (mev).
- The heart is capable of total surrender. If this were not possible, then God would not command us to love the Lord with our whole heart.
- Our first experience with salvation takes place in the heart. We believe in our heart and then confess with our mouth (Rom. 10:9).
- Psalm 119:11 says, "Your word I have hidden in my heart, that I might not sin against You" (mev). The heart is a hiding place, a storage bin, a treasure chest.

As we discussed earlier, the heart has the capability to think. Proverbs 23:7 says that as a man thinks in his heart, so is he. It doesn't say as a man thinks in his head; no, it says as a man thinks in his heart! That's why we must diligently keep watch over our hearts, because as I said in chapter 2, the heart has its own brain.

Thus we really do live from the inside out! It's time to wash the inside of the cup. It's time for a *brain wash*!

Satan's Weapon of Choice

Now, because the heart is such a vital part to our spiritual and emotional well-being, there's an enemy who wants a piece of the action. He wants a place. Ephesians 4:27 says, "Neither give place to the devil" (kjv). We believers need to wise up and do everything possible to keep our hearts a dirt-free zone, because we don't want the enemy to set up his base of operations on Christ's territory. Satan wants to control the epicenter of our life to get it spinning out of control. His weapon of choice to set our lives on the wrong trajectory is the weapon of offense.

This weapon gets the award for most successfully crippling God's people. It's what has brought so many of God's people to a standstill. It's the number one cause of Christians falling away and going AWOL—all because their hearts were left unguarded and offense therefore took root.

In Matthew 18:21–35 Peter asks Jesus if forgiving a brother or sister who sinned against him seven times is enough. Under the requirement of the law, the rabbis taught that people should forgive only three times. Peter was going way over the top by suggesting that we forgive seven times. (I wonder if one of the other disciples was getting on Peter's nerves. After all, they did travel around together and were placed in very stressful situations at times, to say the least.) Well, just when we think we have it all figured out, nice and neatly packaged, Jesus always tells us a more excellent way (such as to turn the other cheek and go the extra mile).

Jesus answers Peter, "No, Pete. Seven times is nowhere near enough." That number is almost laughable compared to what Jesus had in mind. He told Peter we should forgive seventy times seven! The point wasn't the number. Jesus wasn't saying that once we've forgiven a person 490 times, we can wash our hands of them. No! The lesson Jesus was trying to teach was that we must forgive that person as often as he or she needs our forgiveness, just as we have been forgiven—let off the hook—for our debt and are able to walk away scot free, owing nothing. To do anything less would mean that the condition of our hearts and the condition of the hearts of the people who need forgiveness will be compromised, and our hearts will become fertile ground for the enemy to cause division among those whom God loves.

In Matthew 18 Jesus tells a parable that clearly shows that we all owe a tremendous debt that we could never pay. That debt would have been attached to our family and all that we own. In the parable a merciful king who was owed a huge debt wanted to settle accounts, so he decided to wipe the slate clean and allow the debtor and his family to walk away scot free with all his possessions. The only requirement this merciful king had was that the debtor would pay it forward. He would do unto others as it was done unto him.

The parable goes on to say that someone owed the forgiven debtor a much lesser amount, but this proud man didn't realize what had been done for him. This man represents people just like us, who often suffer from spiritual amnesia and hold on to offenses because we want the offender to pay for whatever wrong was done to us. We somehow feel that *we* deserve forgiveness, yet others don't deserve the same treatment.

This kind of attitude doesn't fare well with merciful Jesus. In the parable Jesus is more upset at the unmerciful forgiven guy than the person who owed him money. The man who offended the forgiven guy begged just as the forgiven man had begged the merciful king, but the forgiven man wouldn't forgive. *Wow!* The forgiven man was only looking at what was owed to him instead of what he now owed his servant. He owed his servant the same mercy he was shown.

The only way the merciful king could teach this unmerciful guy a lesson was to lock him up to be tortured until he paid back what he owed. Could it be that what he owed was to just forgive the debt of his brother? To just release him totally, just as he had been released?

The fact is, until we totally forgive, we are all bound up inside, tortured and imprisoned. It is also true that when we forgive, we are freed from the inner prison of self-righteousness, revenge, and the need to gossip. Jesus said the only way to forgive is *from the heart* (Matt. 18:35)! Yes, *from the heart*, not *from the head!* In Matthew 18:35 Jesus said that's how His heavenly Father forgives—it's *heart forgiveness*, not *head forgiveness!* When we forgive in our head and not our heart, the old emotions that stem from our hearts for being wronged keep washing away the thoughts in our minds that tell us it is absolutely right to forgive.

But our minds really have very little power to forgive. Once we forgive *in the heart*, the whole landscape of our being is changed. Now the thoughts that creep into our minds have no leg to stand on because the temperature of the heart has been melted by the knowledge that we absolutely in no way, shape, or form deserve to be forgiven or to receive new mercies every single morning. But we receive them anyway because God has forgiven us from His heart. We also know from the Lord's Prayer that unless we forgive, we won't be forgiven. It's as simple as that!

Jesus, knowing how deadly holding on to offense is, says in Matthew 5:23–24: "Therefore, if you are offering your gift at the altar and *there remember that your brother or sister has something against you,* leave your gift there in front of the altar. First go and be reconciled to them; then come and offer your gift" (emphasis added). Notice that He doesn't say if you have something against your brother, nor does He say it's OK to forgive when you get the chance. No, He said to leave your gift *there* in front of the altar and *go and be reconciled* to your brother immediately—ASAP!— and then come back and offer your gift.

Jesus is asking His disciples to take the initiative in the process of reconciliation—whether they were in the wrong or not. Not only are we guardians of our own hearts, but also God wants to make sure that as long as it is possible, we are to keep our brothers' and sisters' hearts a dirt-free zone. You truly are your brother's keeper! That is God's standard.

Be Quick To Mend Fences

I can tell you what the church's standard is, but let me make it more personal. Let me tell you what my standard has unfortunately been in past years. Allow me to paint a picture for you.

I am in the middle of hot, passionate worship with the Lord—tears falling, arms swaying—and there I remember that a certain person has been acting differently toward me lately. I think (in my heart, of course), "I wonder what's wrong with Sister So-and-So? What's up with her? Why is she acting so distant and weird toward me? Well, that's her problem . . . " All the while I'm singing "I Surrender All" at the top of my lungs. Ah, there's the dust ball, all because I didn't do things according to "code," or according to God's Word. I didn't go and remove it as soon as I realized there was a breach. Instead I did what so many others have been doing for centuries. I swept it under the rug, and it just collected more and more dust in my heart as time went on.

I cohabited the same church building with her, worshipping the same God, but I made sure I never sat on the same side of the church as she did. I also knew which aisle she frequented and what door she exited, so I avoided those areas to steer clear of any drama. Then one day the inevitable happened: our paths crossed. We immediately acted as though we didn't see each other and avoided eye contact.

I just happened to be with one of my close friends, and it seemed that rug collecting dust balls couldn't fit another thing under it. I spurted out something like, "I don't know why, but I really don't think she likes me." There it was—the dust ball just snowballed! Now someone else became part of a situation that definitely could have been avoided. Of course, my friend told another friend, and the list of people brought into the conflict grew. At that point we had little pockets of division and the beginning of cliques, which is so opposite of what God's will is for His people.

Doesn't it say in Psalm 133 that where there is unity, that's where the Lord's blessing is? Doesn't it say how good and pleasant it is when we, God's people, dwell together in unity? Unity in the body of Christ, both the local and universal body of believers, is very precious and should be protected at all costs. Unity causes the anointing to flow down from heaven onto the congregation. Unity is the catalyst for revival. Unity knits us together so tightly the enemy can't creep into our midst and destroy our fellowship. True fellowship is so delightful and delicious. So suffice it to say that disunity doesn't make for a pleasant visit to the house of the Lord, because God's presence isn't as present as it could be.

Could it be that disunity is so jarring, not even the Holy Spirit wants to be around it? Could it be that the one little dust ball left unchecked can snowball and eventually be responsible for the dilution of God's presence in our midst? If we treasure the move of the Holy Spirit, then we must be intentional about guarding the unity of the brethren *at all costs*!

You see, when we do things God's way, it kills two egos with one stone. Doing things God's way keeps both parties in check. When we don't heed God's Word, we are probably "pride-walking" instead of "power-walking." The Bible says in Ephesians 4:3, "Make every effort to keep the unity of the Spirit through the bond of peace." Paul calls it an effort, which means it's not easy. He also states that the Holy Spirit brings the unity, but it's our responsibility to keep it. We keep it through the bond of peace, or as *The Message* puts it, we are to be "quick at mending fences"!

We ought to be fanatics about our unity. Jesus was certainly passionate about it. His last prayer before He went off to be tortured for all our sin was, "That all of them may be one, Father, just as you are in me and I am in you. May they also be in us *so that the world may believe that you have sent me*" (John 17:21, emphasis added). Here Jesus is praying, "Father, make them a unified front." Unity is tangible to the senses; where there is unity, there is order and peace. Disunity is also tangible, but it is very off-putting.

Recently my husband was invited to be a part of the Night of Hope at Yankee Stadium, where Pastors Joel and Victoria Osteen spoke to 55,000 people. My husband and twelve other pastors stood on this great platform, and each one was given a declaration of hope to speak out concerning a particular topic or area. My husband was asked to pronounce hope over our government and nation. He said that the sense of God on that platform was overwhelming. All those pastors joined together from different denominations, and though they had different styles of worship and leadership, they set all those differences aside to lift up and serve the same God. My husband said that you could sense the unity and the power that came from that united front.

Wow! Can you now see why the enemy wants to set us against one another? Can you see why the enemy has caused division and discord among denominations? Can you see how we become nothing but pawns in the enemy's hands when we don't do things God's way? I hope you can now see that the little skirmishes we face on a daily basis really have very little to do with us and are really an attempt to prevent the Holy Spirit from showing up and displaying His power! If we want to keep the enemy from succeeding in this, we must allow the thoughts in our hearts to get on the same page as the One who lives inside our hearts. He must have the run of our house.

Let's Pray

Lord, please allow my heart to be in line with Your Word. Please allow my heart to be humbled in Your presence, knowing that as You have forgiven me, I must quickly forgive others. Please keep my heart from being a place where the enemy is able to set up his base of operations. Rather, may my heart be a base of operations for the Holy Spirit to dismantle disunity in the body of Christ by my love and graciousness toward others. Teach me what it really means to forgive from my heart. I want my heart to be pleasing in Your sight, dear Lord. In Jesus's name, amen.

Maria Durso

CHAPTER 7 – HEART ATTACKS

N o one—and I mean no one—is exempt from being offended. Remember John the Baptist? You may be thinking, "Surely not him. Someone who eats locusts and honey and dresses in camel's hair is surely past the point of being offended. He was one committed dude—magna cum laude in the halls of religious excellence as far as I'm concerned!" But unfortunately offense happens to the best of the best!

In Matthew 11:2–3 the Bible says that when John was in prison, he heard about the things Jesus was doing, and he sent his disciples to ask Him, "Are you the one who is to come, or should we expect someone else?" Can you imagine? John, who saw the dove descend upon Jesus's head and simultaneously heard a voice from heaven say, "This is My beloved Son, in whom I am well pleased," suddenly isn't sure that Jesus is the promised Messiah. He had a moment of doubt and voiced it by sending his disciples to question Jesus.

Now, I think that if I saw a dove descend on Jesus and heard a voice from heaven saying Jesus was His beloved Son, that would be all I'd need to be convinced. But when God isn't doing what we expect Him to do for us at the present time, in our present circumstances, offense can easily slip right in, and we can start to question the sovereignty of God. I believe that's what happened with John. He was in prison, and Isaiah 61 clearly states that the Messiah came to set the prisoner free. Why wasn't Jesus setting John free? After all, he fit the criteria. He was in prison, he was doing God's will, and he was Jesus's cousin to boot!

I wonder if John's imprisonment affected his parents, Elizabeth and Zechariah. I wonder if it caused a rift between them and their cousins Mary and Joseph. Perhaps that's why Jesus said in Luke 7:23, "Blessed is he who is not offended because of Me" (nkjv).

How often have we been offended because of what God has allowed to happen to us or because of what He didn't allow to happen to us? Failed expectations and disappointments are a great source of offense.

In Luke 17:1 Jesus is having a conversation with His disciples— His peeps. He's warning them about events that can happen on any given day and that have the potential to trip them up. He wants to prepare them so they will know how to handle these situations when they occur. Notice I said *when* they occur, not if.

Please allow me to paraphrase and embellish Luke 17:1 a bit. Jesus is saying, "Listen, fellas, it is simply unthinkable that you could live this life without being offended—unless you live on Mount Kilimanjaro or in a cave or in a house alone and you never answer your doorbell or your phone.

This is a definite. You can take it to the bank. Offenses will come. And guys, here's a little more bad news: not only is offense inevitable, but it's also going to happen often. And if that's not bad enough, it's going to happen between brothers and sisters, people close to you in the church community. And to add insult to injury, God allows it."

Jesus doesn't say, "Offense will come, but don't worry; I'll protect you." Or, "Offenses will come but *not* to My people." *Nope.* Offense is an equal-opportunity frustration. The good news is that God is an equal-opportunity distributor of supernatural defense against it.

How we handle offense is the litmus test of our spiritual maturity. It seems in John 17:1 that Jesus is saying offense comes without warning, sort of like a heart attack. Yes, that's what offense is precisely—an attack on the heart!

The word *offense* comes from the Greek word *skandalon*, which is where we get the word *scandal* or *scandalous*. It seems to suggest something mischievous, premeditated, and deceptive. As it would happen, *skandalon* also describes a small, unassuming block of wood that keeps a trapdoor to a cage open. Bait specific to the intended target is placed inside the cage; for example, cheese is placed inside for a mouse and nuts for a squirrel. The bait is tailored to lure the right victim. The target accidentally knocks into the *skandalon*, or the block of wood or "stumbling block," and suddenly the door slams shut, trapping the victim inside.[1]

So do you think it is safe to say that offense is a setup, a lure, a snare, a trap, a stumbling block that suddenly blindsides us, entrapping us in a cage of negative emotions? The enemy's goal is to cage us in bitterness and resentment. If we allow ourselves to be entrapped by offense, he will have us where he wants us. Because we are trapped, we can't see farther than the cage permits, and we have to eat what's being fed to us.

When offense is not properly dealt with, the offended usually becomes the offender. The bitten becomes the biter. That's why Jesus says in Luke 17:3, "*Watch yourselves*" (emphasis added). He's saying, "Guard your heart. Don't worry about the offender. I'll take care of him." After all, He said in Luke 17:1, "Woe to anyone through whom [offenses] come." But please, guys, remember that each of us must keep a clean heart at all costs. If you think being hurt by someone you love is bad, just wait till you see what bitterness and resentment will do to you.

Not only will offense destroy your peace, but it will also totally change who you are. It will affect and infect your anointing. Offense is like having a leech inside your heart. It will suck out your anointing and purpose and drain all your strength and creativity. Speaking from experience, I can tell you that if you let offense contaminate your heart, every word you speak and every decision you make will be filtered through the lens of offense. Keep your heart clean, because your life choices are at stake!

Destroyed By Offense

Proverbs 18:19 says, "A brother offended is harder to be won than a strong city" (mev). In other words, it's easier to get inside a city that's barricaded with armored guards than to reach someone who has been offended. Let's look throughout the Bible to see how holding on to offense wrecked the call of God on so many people. These individuals had great potential to change their surroundings, but instead they caused great destruction, all because of offense.

Absalom

Second Samuel 13 tells the story of Absalom's downfall into the trap of offense. His half-brother Amnon raped Absalom's sister Tamar, and their father, David, did *nothing!* Deep offense comes when we feel unprotected by our parents or the people who are supposed to shelter us. From the day Amnon raped Tamar, Absalom never moved on. He was stuck in the land of offense. He had the potential to be a great influencer, but he ended up causing great division and chaos in his father's kingdom. It is important to note that *Absalom was accidentally hanged!* (See 2 Samuel 18:9–10.)

Ahithophel

Second Samuel 16 tells us the story of Ahithophel, who was David's closest advisor. The Bible says he spoke as the oracle of God. Some commentators believe that Ahithophel was the grandfather of Uriah, Bathsheba's husband. David slept with Bathsheba when Uriah was off to war, and Bathsheba became pregnant. To cover his tracks, David had Uriah killed. Deep offense comes when our king, our pastor, our leader doesn't practice what he preaches. After Uriah was killed, Ahithophel hooked up with Absalom, who rebelled against his father. Isn't it amazing how offended people usually join forces? Ahithophel, who was once the oracle of God, became the mouthpiece of Satan. It is important to note that *Ahithophel hanged himself!* (See 2 Samuel 17:23.)

Judas

At the beginning of John 12 it is six days before the Passover and Jesus is invited to be the guest of honor at the home of Martha, Mary, and Lazarus. There is going to be a great celebration because Lazarus was brought back from the dead, and Jesus brings His disciples. During the dinner Mary unexpectedly takes out a pint of ointment, worth a year's wages, and pours it on Jesus's feet. The Bible says that Judas became indignant. He was offended by Mary's actions.

Why in the world would Mary's pouring perfume on Jesus's feet offend Judas? Well, I thought long and hard about this, and then it struck me: Judas was the treasurer. He was in charge of anything valuable—everybody knew that! He constantly carried that money bag on his side. Being the treasurer was his identity! How dare this Mary, this woman, this layperson who wasn't even an apostle, bypass him and go straight to Jesus! How dare she not ask Judas's permission or his opinion about how the expensive ointment would best be used!

Mary's actions didn't fall in line with protocol, and I believe Judas's pride was bruised. He was now caught in the trap of offense, but he disguised it in a spiritual casing, as we oftentimes do. He said, "Why wasn't this perfume sold and the money given to the poor?" (See verse 5.) Then Jesus replied with the words that slammed the cage door shut: "Leave her alone. What she did was ordered by God!" (See John 12:7.) *Whoa*—that's the last thing you want to hear when you're offended.

Deep offense comes when we feel disrespected. How many times have we been offended by the actions of someone on our ministry team? Maybe we were overlooked or bypassed. Maybe someone else got the solo. Maybe another brother was asked to be on the executive team. Maybe all your hard work wasn't mentioned in the bulletin, but Sister So-and-So received a huge acknowledgment and all she did was make a Bundt cake. What's so hard about making a cake with a hole in the middle? Be careful not to allow pride and the need for recognition to trap you in a cage of offense. Take my word for it: when we do things for recognition, because the Holy Spirit loves us so much He makes sure we don't get any!

In the next chapter we will see how the offended becomes the offender, just as Absalom and Ahithophel did. But for now let's see how the enemy used offense to trap Judas. The Bible says that the devil put into the *heart* of Judas—the *unguarded heart* of Judas— the thought to betray Jesus. See, now the devil has taken Judas captive to do his will. Judas then betrays Christ, betrays his call, forfeits his anointing, and *hangs himself!* (See Matthew 27:5.)

Hanging on to offense is spiritual suicide. Hanging on to offense prevents God's Spirit from working in us, and it hinders His Spirit from moving in our midst! Judas finally received the recognition he wanted from the grimy religious leaders, but once he got what he thought he wanted, he realized how empty it was. He was looking for recognition from the wrong source.

The Sycamine Tree

Let's go back to the conversation Jesus was having in Luke 17. In verses 4 and 5 Jesus tells His disciples that no matter how many times they are offended, they have to keep on forgiving. After Jesus says this, the disciples cry out, "Help! Increase our faith!" This is the only time they ever asked for an increase of faith. I think that's because they realized it's easier to raise the dead than to forgive when you are offended.

The toughest test you will ever face as a Christian is when you are taken advantage of, overlooked, or falsely accused. Jesus told His disciples that they didn't need more faith; they just needed genuine faith (v. 6). It could be as small as a mustard seed, but their faith must be genuine. To me, "genuine faith" is wanting God's will over what my feelings dictate. Here's a key: if you genuinely want to be free from offense, you can rise up, take authority, and tell that offense rooted deep down in your heart to be uprooted.

In verse 6 Jesus draws a parallel to the sycamine tree. Is it a coincidence that He starts the conversation in Luke 17 talking about *skandalon*, thus likening offense to a small, unassuming block of wood, and ends the conversation speaking about one of the largest, weightiest trees there was at the time? The small offense has become something massive!

Isn't that how the enemy works? He gets his foot in the door, and before you know it, there's a takeover. The door is opened through a tiny offense and it becomes hard to shut, and then it seems the enemy has his fingers on the control panel of your life. No longer led by the Holy Spirit, you are dragged into mental arguments and conversations that cloud your judgment.

The sycamine tree wasn't a random pick. It was known to have the most complicated root system. Rabbis believed it would take six hundred years to untangle the roots. Six hundred years was the life expectancy of the tree. Imagine that. It would take six or seven lifetimes to untangle the roots!

Wow! This tree was so unusual because it grew and thrived best in dry conditions. The sycamine tree produced the bitterest figs, and its wood was used to make caskets. Jesus knew that when offense is not dealt with, it has the same potential as that tree. It is weighty, massive, and complicated. Offense outlives us and can be handed down from generation to generation. Roots of offense entangle every area of our lives, and they are extremely hard to kill. When we are offended, we thrive in dryness, we produce bitter fruit, and we are surrounded by death. I believe Jesus wanted His disciple to know, "You'd better deal with something small before it becomes something major."

Speaking from experience, I can tell you that once your heart is offense-free, it cannot be left unguarded. There's only one other block of wood, only one other tree that could guard the heart and keep it offense-free. There's only one other massive, weighty tree that can counteract the massive, weighty tree of offense, and that's *Calvary's tree*! This tree surrounds us with life and not death. It is the tree that resurrects instead of buries. It breaks generational curses instead of causing them. It causes our fruit to be sweet and not bitter. This tree plants us in the soil of forgiveness.

When Calvary's tree is front and center, it becomes impossible to hang on to offense because the innocent Lamb of God hung on a splintered block of wood. He did that willingly for me and for you. If we contrast what was done for us with what was done to us, the offense won't compare to the debt Jesus paid for us to clear the sum total of all our sins. We have a choice today: forgive and let it go, or *hang on* and let it grow! When we forget what Jesus did for us by *hanging* on the cross, we *hang* on to the offense, and the rest of our lives will *hang* in the balance.

Allow me to end this critical chapter with a dream I had that was absolutely life changing. A number of years ago there were two women in our church whom I loved dearly and considered very close friends, even sisters. These women ended up teaming up and criticizing our church—the church that I know they loved and were a vital part of—causing division. This devastated me, and I became fearful to trust people. I was trapped. The cage door had slammed shut, and everything I did and said was through the lens of offense. I needed a *brain wash*!

In the dream I was having a knock-down, drag-out fight with one of these women. This was the way I handled things before I got saved (and for a little while afterward also!). Of course, because it was my dream, I was winning. I had her against the wall, punching her and pulling her hair. As I got her down to the ground, I started screaming, "I'm winning! I'm winning!" Just then I clearly heard the Holy Spirit speak to me. He said, "Are you really winning, Maria?" Then He said, "Don't wake up until you are laying hands on her, praying for her and blessing her."

It seemed like I stayed sleeping for hours and hours more. I just couldn't get the words out. I didn't want to bless her and let her off the hook. Finally I started to lay my hands on her the right way, and I began to pray down blessings. The more I prayed down blessings on her, the more I felt released. The cage door opened, and I was *free*! When I woke up, I realized that was a small price to pay for freedom. I got up and made a list of all the people I had ought against in my heart. I made it a practice to pray down blessings upon them every day until I had nothing left in my heart against them. I was clean—squeaky clean.

Jesus's words really are the way out. He said to pray for your enemies and bless those who "despitefully use you" (Matt. 5:44, kjv). Whenever I read that, I wouldn't quite do it His way. I would pray for them, but in my offended heart, I was really saying let them get hit by a car or something awful like that. I never wanted them to die—I was way too spiritual for that! I just wanted them to feel pain, because I was in pain. When I heard that forgiveness is not only for the one in need of forgiveness but also probably more for the one who needs to forgive, I couldn't see how that could possibly be true. Now I know forgiving is truly a matter of life or death, success or failure!

Ladies and gentlemen, if you want to lose weight, *forgive* from your heart—you will feel one hundred pounds lighter! Your heart that is enlarged because it's filled with hatred and revenge will instead be filled with love and graciousness for others. Wow, that's really taking the weight off. Also, if you want to build spiritual muscle, go against the grain and *forgive big!* This is the real test of our spiritual maturity and character development. Muscle building doesn't just "happen"; you have to pick up weights that stress the muscle out. Dealing with the "weighty matters" of the heart is what grows us up and causes us to become mature giants in the faith.

How about you? Is it time for your heart to be washed? Would you say, "Lord, give me a *brain wash* in my heart"? I hope so. You are just eighteen inches from growing up into a person the Lord wants to put in the big leagues!

Let's Pray

Dear Lord, I want to be all that You have called me to be, and I certainly don't want my anointing to be infected with the disease of offense-itis. I don't want to live in the land of offense, but I want to live in the land of the living. I want my feet to climb to higher heights as my heart is set free to soar. So I release the weights that have held my heart down one by one. Free Your servant, Lord. Let it be done unto me according to Thy Word, and may Your kingdom come down and explode in my heart on earth as it is in heaven. In Jesus's name, amen.

Maria Durso

CHAPTER 8 – COMPLEXES . . . WILL THEY EVER GO AWAY?

Not too long ago the world mourned the untimely death of Whitney Houston. It was tragic. The media focused on her rise to fame and her fall from the pinnacle of greatness. She was one of the most beautiful, gifted, graceful singers of her time, but she battled addiction for many years. Many have blamed drugs for her death, because she was found dead of an overdose. But were drugs really her downfall, or was the drug abuse caused by something much deeper?

What could have brought down this woman who was raised up in the ways of the Lord and who knew God's Word? What could have destroyed her spirit? I was fixated on the television in the days after her death, as was the rest of the world. I listened intently to every interview, to every friend and relative who spoke about her life. In every interview replayed, I studied her facial expressions and her eyes, which are the window to the soul. I wanted to know what had brought this magnificent singer down.

Around the same time I saw an interview with Lady Gaga that was being conducted in the halls of Madison Square Garden, where she was to perform. The cameras scanned the thousands of "little monsters" as they poured inside the venue to see her perform. But back in her dressing room Lady Gaga was in tears as she told an interviewer that she sometimes feels like a loser.

"It's crazy because it's like we're at the Garden, but I still sometimes feel like a loser kid in high school," she said. "I just got to . . . pick myself up and I have to tell myself I'm a superstar every morning so that I can get through this day and be for my fans what they need for me to be. . . . I just want to be a queen for them, and sometimes I don't feel like one."[1]

As the cameras zoomed in, you could clearly see the deep pain in her eyes. It was the same look I saw in Whitney's eyes. As a matter of fact, it was the same look that I've seen in the eyes of thousands upon thousands of women. Unfortunately it's the same look I've seen in my own eyes as they stared back at me in the mirror.

I thought, "Here we have two totally different women, with two totally different upbringings, from two totally different ethnic backgrounds performing two totally different styles of music. But maybe they're not that different at all. Maybe their similarities are greater than their differences."

Lady Gaga has said that she was bullied as a young girl,[2] and from the look in her eyes I got the sense that she would trade all her fame and fortune in a New York minute just to have not suffered through those painful times. It was as though she wasn't satisfied with who she was. Even though she was one of the top entertainers at that time, from the look in her eyes she did not like being her. She might have loved where she was, but she didn't seem to love who she was. She didn't seem to be comfortable in her own skin.

Whitney's friends seemed to suggest that she shared those sentiments. They said that she would wonder, "Am I good enough?" "Am I pretty enough?" "Will they like me?"[3] These singers' complexes seemed to have sabotaged their joy. It's as though they had a spike or thorn in their flesh, pricking them and causing them great distress as an accusatory finger constantly pointed at their minor defects instead of their great accomplishments.

Complexes—they're complex. They define us way down on the inside. They shape how we see ourselves. They are always with us. We can't leave them at home. They follow us around like Mary's little lamb. We wonder if other people see them. And although they shouldn't, these complexes overshadow nearly everything we do. Even the great singer Barbra Streisand had them. She once forgot the words to a song in the middle of a performance and avoided singing live for more than twenty years. *Wow!*

Complexes. We all have them. I don't believe there's a person on the planet who doesn't feel flawed in some way, shape, or form. Flawed because of an imperfection. Flawed because of some rejection. Flawed because of some stinging memory, some insensitive putdown, some disappointment, some failure, some imperfection that stares back at you in the mirror.

In 2 Corinthians 12 the Bible deals with such things. The apostle Paul speaks of weaknesses caused by a thorn in his flesh. One of the definitions of the word translated "weakness" in 2 Corinthians 12:9 is distressing, unsettling emotions.[4] It would stand to reason that distressing emotions could cause a person to feel fainthearted, weak, or needy. The apostle Paul admitted that he too had weaknesses, frailties, and deep, unsettling emotions. His came from a thorn in his flesh sent by Satan to buffet him (v. 7). The Greek word translated "thorn" in verse 7 means something that causes severe pain or constant irritation.[5] Many believe it was a physical ailment such as an eye disease, but I believe Paul was emotionally tormented. I believe Satan wanted to throw Paul off his game, to discourage and torment him.

I believe Paul's thorn was not only in the form of difficult people who would try his patience and torture him, but it was also an internal thorn that challenged the call of God on His life. But we know that anything the enemy throws at us, God will use for His benefit. Later in this chapter I will address why God allows such things and how He uses them for His benefit.

Drawn To The Scars

Strangely enough, our imperfections often are the very things that cause others to identify with us. Aren't we usually more attracted to people who are willing to be real and show us their weakness than to those who seem to be perfect? Isn't it easier to relate to people with scars just like ours? I think the church should recognize this. We try so hard to appear perfect to outsiders that we often seem plastic and not human. We spout scriptures at people, but we can't help them where they're at because we want to pretend we never had a past and act like we can't relate to them. We act like we never have a bad day, never have a bad thought, like we would never lose our tempers and could never lose our minds at any given moment if it weren't for God's grace!

I think oftentimes we don't want to let God down. We want to be His perfect little soldiers, His perfect little sons and daughters. And we certainly don't want to be judged by our fellow brothers and sisters. But maybe the most spiritual thing we could do is to be totally honest, down and dirty, transparent and vulnerable. What we need to do is find some people who feel like they will never be up to snuff and tell them about our struggles, fears, and the insecurities we still deal with. Tell them we are under construction. Tell them we are not what we want to be but certainly a long way from what we used to be. If we were to do that, I believe it would be tremendous encouragement for their souls.

I'll tell you who else is attracted to weakness. That would be God. God uses imperfect people—flawed people. He said He uses the foolish things to confound the wise (1 Cor. 1:27). Imagine that. God uses the things society mocks to baffle and confuse them—and to baffle and confuse us at the same time. I've heard it preached that D.L. Moody had a complex because he was uneducated.[6] And I've read that the highly educated orator Charles Spurgeon suffered from deep, unsettling emotions.[7] Many times they wanted to throw in the towel. More times than not they were dissatisfied with their sermons, which blinded them from seeing the massive number of souls they had won to the Lord. But they're not the only ones. There are several figures in the Bible who clearly must have wrestled with complexes.

The apostle Paul said, "For I am the least of the apostles and am not fit to be called an apostle, because I persecuted the church of God" (1 Cor. 15:9, mev). *The Message* puts it this way: "I don't deserve to be included in that inner circle, as you well know, having spent all those early years trying my best to stamp God's church right out of existence." He had a complex. He wrestled with the belief that because of his past deeds, he didn't deserve his current position.

I'm almost positive that every time Paul got a tremendous revelation, the thorn that pierced his self-confidence screamed inside of him, saying, "Who do you think you are?" Yet the Holy Spirit used Paul to write most of the New Testament, complexes and all.

How about Joshua? I bet he had a forty-year complex after he was given the reins to lead the Israelites into the Promised Land. Can you imagine what Joshua was really thinking when the captain of the Lord's host appeared to Him in Joshua 5:13–15? He must have thought, "How in the world am I going to be a leader now when I couldn't convince them forty years ago that we should move forward? Do you remember that after my big, anointed speech, not only did they want to go back to Egypt, but they also wanted to stone me? Well, *I* certainly didn't forget. As a matter of fact, this has put a dent in my leadership skills and has crushed my confidence! I certainly don't think I'm your guy." (See Numbers 14:1–11.)

Let's face it, would you hire someone with that track record to be the CEO of your company? I think not; but as you know, God doesn't think even remotely like that. He gets a kick out of getting us to do things that our hearts and minds tell us we could never do. That's why we need a brain wash! Maybe that's why God had to tell Joshua over and over again, "Do not be afraid." It has been said that "Do not fear" is written 365 times in Scripture. That means there is a "fear not" for every day of the year!

And how about David? He definitely must have had complexes! Some Bible commentators believe he was an illegitimate son. There is no mention of his mother in the genealogy. He was given the job of a shepherd, the lowest position on the totem pole. His own father didn't bring him in from the fields. He wasn't even a consideration to be king, just an afterthought!

Even the prophet Samuel got it wrong (1 Sam. 16:1–13). Man, talk about adding insult to injury! Samuel thought tall, dark, and handsome Eliab was God's man. I bet everyone always thought Eliab was the man, certainly not the young, ruddy shepherd boy David! You know the stereotype of whom God can use and whom He can't. Can God use someone who is illegitimate? Can God use someone young? Of course!

Man alive, I can so relate to David! When a building was given to the Brooklyn Tabernacle, the church started to pray, "Lord, raise up a team." Never in a billion zillion years would I ever have thought God would choose my husband and me. We didn't come from a Christian background. We came from a background of drugs and divorce. Some people may be thinking, "Not *divorce*! Not the *d-word*!" Oh, yes, *divorce*! Maybe God forgot the small fact that we were divorced. Doesn't He have that short-term memory thing going on with Him dropping things in that big sea of forgetfulness?

According to some denominations, we could never be used because of the divorce in our pasts. We'd be considered damaged goods forever! But the Holy Spirit showed Pastor Jim Cymbala and the elders of Brooklyn

Tabernacle that we were the ones to lead this team. Not only were *we* shocked, but also you should have seen the reactions of the other people. They said things like, "You? Really? You guys? Wow!" Nothing like a little encouragement from your peers! Guess who definitely needed a brain wash? Not them, silly goose—*me!* I definitely needed a brain wash!

David's daddy, Jesse, needed a brain wash too. After he saw Samuel anoint his son in front of the whole family, he obviously didn't embrace David's new status. In 1 Samuel 17 he sent David out as a delivery boy to take his brothers some lunch. Instead of bullets, blades, and bombs, Jesse gave David a basket of bread and cheese. Instead of sending him out as an anointed king, as God's man, Jesse sent David out as "little red riding hood"! That's manly and kingly! How humiliating. When David walked onto the battlefield, Eliab mocked him, Saul laughed at him, and Goliath scorned him. Talk about a bad ministry day! David definitely needed a brain wash!

Lessons From David

In the midst of this humiliation David did several things that I believe were very significant to his future success, things that can teach us how to handle the curveballs life often throws at us.

David laid down his burden.

Let's picture David walking, carrying a basket of humiliation that symbolized how his father viewed him and reinforced the label the devil wanted to stamp on him: *loser!* David had to choose whether to keep going forward or listen to the voice of the enemy that was screaming with every step: "Go home, David, go home. You don't belong here! You are way out of your league." But the Bible says that as soon as David walked on the battlefield, he left the things he was carrying with the keeper of the supplies (1 Sam. 17:22). This tells me that if we want to place our foot on the battlefield, we have to be unencumbered, unhindered, and unobstructed. We can't be successful fighting the battle if we are weighed down with the things people put on us. We have to leave our weights with the One who carries all our burdens!

David ignored the taunts.

When David arrived at the battlefront, his brother Eliab immediately attacked him: "Why are you here? With whom did you leave those few sheep? I know how wicked your heart is and how conceited you are. Go home, David, go home." (See 1 Samuel 17:28.) *Wow!* How do you recover from that? This was a perfect opportunity for David to spit in his brother's sandwich! But the Bible says David turned away and spoke about the matter to someone else (v. 30). In other words, he didn't even qualify Eliab's comments. It was as though he said without really saying it, "Talk to the hand, Eliab!" When people try to discourage and accuse you, don't defend yourself—and don't internalize it either. This is key. Turn away and keep going forward. Always remember, God is your defender!

David stayed true to himself.

When David finally reached King Saul, Saul laughed at him, demeaning him and saying, "You are only a boy." But Saul finally gave in to a determined David and said, "OK, boy. If you insist on going out there and fighting that giant, put my armor on." So David put the armor on and clinked and clanked around the king's tent. He could have thought, "Go home, David, go home. You don't fit in the big boys' clothes." *But David didn't go home!* Instead he said, "I can't go in this armor," and he took it off. (See 1 Samuel 17:33, 38–39.) This tells me we all have our own armor. We don't need to wear anyone else's. Just be yourself. You have your own style. As long as you take off the giant's head, who cares what method you use? It may be behind a pulpit or it may be in the mall; you may wear a suit and tie or jeans and a hoodie—who cares? Just swing the Rock, Christ Jesus—and carry it around as a reminder that it's only the Rock who slays the giants that stand in our path!

David and Paul certainly weren't the only biblical figures who dealt with complexes. How about the Shulamite woman, Solomon's beloved in the Song of Songs? Talk about complexes. She had to work in her brothers' vineyards, and as a result her skin was not delicate; it was neither fair nor smooth. She didn't have the luxury of having facials or applying the rich emollients that were used by the daughters of Jerusalem. When the king came along, he was smitten with her, ashy skin and all. And what do you think she did? Well, I'll tell you what she didn't do: she didn't accept his accolades. She started to point out all her flaws instead of accepting the affection he was lavishing upon her. Boy, I can so relate to her. We need to learn to accept compliments without having the need to sabotage them by putting ourselves down.

And what about poor Sarah, who used to be Sarai? She had to change her name to "Mother of Many Nations," and she couldn't even get pregnant. Every time she had to say her name, I bet she turned beet red and proceeded to mumble her new name under her breath. I'm sure she cringed on the inside. I know I definitely would. Isn't that how we all truly feel? God says we are one thing, but that's light-years away from how we really feel.

I don't know how Sarah handled it, but I can tell you how she could have handled it. Every time someone raised an eyebrow (since these were pre-Botox days) as she signed her name or wore her name tag at the women's spring luncheon, she could have felt compelled to tell the *whole* story of how God told her husband to look up and see the stars and know that their children would be just as numerous. She could have told them how God said they'd have a zillion billion children one day! We know from the account in Genesis that Sarah had a hard time believing what God said, but that's not what God wants for us. He wants us to believe we are who He says we are.

Last but not least, let's look at Moses. Moses came from a family of priests, believers in Jehovah God. When Moses was an infant, trouble came to his neighborhood. Pharaoh gave an order to have all the baby boys under three years old annihilated. His mama could not bear to have her baby boy murdered. She placed sweet little Moses in a basket and sent him down the river because she saw that he was no ordinary child, but I can tell you that's *not* how Moses saw himself! We'll get to that in a minute.

Moses ended up in a home that was completely different from his mom and dad's home. (Remember, his birth mother breastfed Moses for three years before Pharaoh's daughter took him to raise as her own.) Moses's parents were slaves. Once his mother weaned him, he had to go live in a different home, in a different culture, with a different dress and belief system. He went from the home of a slave to a palace under the care of Pharaoh's daughter. His old home barely had the necessities of life. The new place had cable, Internet, a pool and pinball machine, servants, spa treatments, and designer robes and sandals!

But all that stuff didn't make up for the fact that Moses felt different. He obviously felt that he didn't fit in. We know he related more to the poor guys than the rich ones. He had absolutely no idea that he had to be in the palace for such a time as this. He had no idea that someday God would use his temporary pain to set his nation free.

Perhaps feeling as though he didn't fit in gave Moses all those anger issues. I wonder if he was teased. Maybe his hair was curly and those in Pharaoh's palace had straight hair. Maybe their skin tones were different. Maybe Moses went through an awkward stage. Maybe he had big ears and acne. Maybe his teeth were crooked. We don't know about any of those things because the Bible is silent concerning them. But one thing we absolutely do know about Moses is that he had slowness of speech. He wasn't quick-tongued. This foster kid, who felt like an alien, had a speech impediment. He stuttered!

Whatever was at the root of his anger, Moses ended up murdering someone and had to flee the palace for his life. The one who was next in line to Pharaoh ended up on the far side of the desert and on Egypt's Most Wanted List! Because of his actions, he closed the one door that was his link to his future. By now you know Moses definitely had a complex. Moses was definitely due for a brain wash!

God's Strength In Our Weakness

The Bible says that one day forty years later, which equals at least 14,600 days later, Moses ended up on the far side of the desert. Commentators say that place is like the dark side of the moon. It can't get any darker or more isolated than that. This is the place where it seems things can't get any worse, the place where it seems things can never change. But, as only God would have it, Moses ended up on Mount Sinai, which is *the mountain of God!*

Who knew that the far side of the desert was right around the corner from the mountain where God resides? This tells me that the desert of despair is right around the corner from the mountain of hope! It also tells me that no matter how far you run, eventually you will run smack-dab into the presence of God! You will run right smack-dab into your destiny!

You probably know the story. The far side of the desert becomes holy ground. The burning bush speaks and calls Moses's name and tells him that God wants to use him. God is going to fulfill the deepest passion that Moses ever had, which was to see his fellow Israelites go free. But this time *God* is going to be the fuel behind the passion, not Moses's anger!

Moses is going to be God's spokesman—not His warrior, not His military general, not His swordsman or a bowman. Nope. Moses is going to be a *spokesman!* A man who stutters is being called to speak! Moses has a hard time grasping what God is saying. He has a hard time absorbing or comprehending that God wants to make public his speech impediment. He with the stammering tongue and faltering lips—the *stutterer is going to be a spokesman!* God wants to put on display the very thing Moses wants to hide.

Being a spokesman is the last thing Moses wants to do. He all but says, "Thanks but no thanks, God! I'd rather hang out here." I'm sure the leper in Matthew 8 didn't want to go back and show himself to the priests. I'm sure the adulterous woman in John 8 didn't want to be an object lesson for the religious leaders. I'm sure the woman at the well in John 4 didn't want to become the town evangelist by going around and saying, "I met a man who told me *everything* about myself!" But you know that is how God rolls!

"Pfa-fa-fa-faroh, Ga-Ga-God sa-sa-sent mmm-mmm-me t-t-to y-you." No way did Moses want to go before Pharaoh! Isn't it incredible that we can have an incredible encounter with God—we can see a bush on fire that speaks and just happens to know our name—but all that can pale in comparison to our complex? *Our thorn.* Our constant source of irritation and conflict. Those deep insecurities that torture us.

The thorn is in opposition to the call and deflates it. The thorn bullies the call. Imagine: the thing Moses desired forty years prior would finally be accomplished, not through his strength but rather through his weakness!

Through his complex—his distressing, unsettling emotions. I'm sure Moses prayed, "God, zap me with the smart gene, the eloquent gene. Make me a swagalicious wordologist—then I'll go and be Your spokesman." When I'm perfect; when I have all the wrinkles ironed out; when I sound like her, speak like him, look good in those shoes, have those gifts, have his influence; when I get my doctorate—then I'll be ready to do whatever You want me to do!

Moses said, "O my Lord. I am not eloquent, neither before nor *since You have spoken to Your servant*" (Exod. 4:10, mev, emphasis added). In other words, "Since we had that 'fiery' conversation, nothing has changed. I'm still stuttering, God! You have forgotten this one minor detail, and here's Your big chance. *Heal me!*" But God basically says to him, "Who gave you your tongue?" (See Exodus 4:11.) And Moses was probably thinking, "My sentiments exactly. *This is what I'm trying to tell You!* You gave me this tongue, so it's up to You to heal it!"

God could have easily healed Moses's tongue, but He didn't. Is God insensitive? No! Here's my point: no matter how much we pray, some things aren't going to be taken away, because what seems great to the world by society's standards may not be so great to God! Charles Spurgeon said that maybe Moses's slowness of speech was better than someone else's quickness of tongue. "Pharaoh had more reason to be afraid of stammering Moses than of the most fluent talker in Egypt."[8]

In his stammer there was power! God basically told Moses, "I'm not going to change your speech, Moe." Just as He told Paul, God said, "The thorn—the complex—stays, because it's in your weakness, in your distressing, unsettling emotions, that My power is made perfect! [See 2 Corinthians 12:9.] My power will anoint your weakness. This is My insurance policy; this will keep you relying on Me."

But God doesn't stop there. He tells Moses what He would change: "See, I have made you a god to Pharaoh" (Exod. 7:1, mev). In other words, God was saying, "*When he sees you, he will see Me. You are Me to Pharaoh! When he hears you, he hears Me! But Moses, here's the deal: when you look at you, you will know that it was I who accomplished it!*" We can't get any deeper than that. We can't muster up any more faith than allowing God to use the very thing we want to hide!

I think our complexes aren't really our issue as much as believing that God can use us despite our complexes. That's why once Paul got a brain wash, he could finally say, "Woohoo! I boast in my weakness, in my complexes, because then and only then is *His power made perfect!*"

Moses asked God, "Who am I?" (Exod. 3:11). God didn't go into Moses's past and explain why he was so messed up. He didn't tell him to take an assessment test to see where his strengths lie. He simply answered, "I'll be with you" (v. 12). In other words, God was saying, "What I have called you to has little to do with you and everything to do with Me."

Moses then asked God, "Who are You?" And God answered,

"I AM that I AM!" (See Exodus 3:13–14.) He was saying, *"I am whatever I need to be at any given time. I am the God who uses the foolish things to confound the wise. I am the God who uses the flawed, the weak, the scarred, the marred, and even the has-been! I am the God who is attracted to weakness, to the unlovely. I am the God who restores the brokenhearted and sends people out after they have failed miserably. I am the God of the second chance!"*

So like Moses, we have to stop despising our weaknesses, because they are really *all* we have to offer! It's time to go the eighteen-inch distance and allow the brains of our hearts to be washed from all our twisted thinking that believes a perfect God wants only perfect vessels. Perfect vessels don't exist; only God is perfect.

We must stop thinking we are the only ones with complexes. Everybody has them. We must settle way down deep in our hearts that we are exactly what God wants to use, so that He alone can receive all the glory and all the honor.

Let's Pray

Dear Lord, please allow me to change the things that I boast about. Let me start to boast in my weaknesses and not my strengths, knowing that it's only in my weaknesses that Your strength is made perfect. Allow me to realize that You would never put me in any place or on any stage without totally covering me with Your anointing. I thank You for Your gracious mercy, and I thank You for every weakness that causes me daily to depend upon You. In Jesus's name, amen.

CHAPTER 9 – THERE IS TREASURE IN THE TRASH

Have you ever wondered if the Lord could ever use your situation or mess? Have you ever thought, "Lord, can You really use *all* my life's experiences, past and present, good and bad—*all* my pain, shame, sufferings, sin, failures, fears, shortcomings, struggles, disappointment, grief, and insecurities? How about my abuse, rebellion, abortion, and divorce? Do You really use *all* things, not just all *good* things?"

I think too often, because we cannot imagine how good could possibly come out of bad, we allow our pain go to waste. Well, I'm here to tell you that our trials, struggles, failures, sin, disappointments, pain, and shame are *recyclable*! Yes, God is in the recycling business. He was the first one to "go green." To recycle is to convert waste into reusable material. We recycle because there are substances in the waste that are redeemable and still have value. In other words, there's more to garbage than meets the eye.

The trash can is not the end; it's just the beginning of a whole new cycle. Long before there were environmentalists, God knew He could create something redeemable out of what seem like life's wasteful moments. From the beginning of time He had a plan in place to repurpose our lives when we lost our purpose. The all seeing God knew that there is treasure in our trash.

There is so much potential in our pain even though we can't immediately see its future value in its present state. Would you believe that some of the backpacks that children carry to school every day were once dirty, old, plastic beverage bottles? Or that some stadium seats were once empty detergent bottles? The new item has absolutely no resemblance to the original. Just by looking at the final recycled product, we'd probably never guess that the items it's made of were once headed for the trash heap. Even stinky manure is turned into the fertilizer that makes our fruit so juicy! In a similar way everything we've gone through or go through can be used for someone else's benefit. Everything in our life can be repurposed to bring comfort and healing to someone else.

In this chapter we are going to take the lid off the trash can and discover the value of what's inside—the things that have just been "going to waste," sitting in the dark corners of our hearts and minds. We're going to get out the hose of God's Word, spray the dirt off our shame, and discover that the events of our past weren't a total waste after all. They're only a waste if we leave them in the garbage can and don't allow the Master to create a masterpiece out of them!

One politician said, "A crisis is a terrible thing to waste." God can squeeze out of our sorrows the oil of gladness for somebody else's life. Think about it: who better than someone who has been given a new lease on life, who has been taken off the trash heap, to minister life to one who is lifeless and needs a second chance?

Before I go on, let me give you a little insight into the way the Holy Spirit gives me revelation. I'm not a natural teacher. Everything I teach comes from things God has revealed to me through everyday events. So please allow me to tell you a true story.

As I was standing at the cash register at my neighborhood health food store, I noticed a small cardboard advertisement that read: "Lanolin—the Ointment. Extracted from the sheared wool of sheep. For centuries used as an aid for dry, cracked skin." Accompanying this small ad were various containers with this ointment. There was a jar that held a thick balm, a bottle filled with an emollient, a tube that held a salve, a pump that contained a moisturizer, and a long, slender bottle filled with pure oil.

I thought to myself, "How could this one substance be administered in so many different forms?" I especially wondered how sheared wool from smelly sheep could become something that provided so much comfort. Now, I'm a visual person, and a little too literal at times, so I sincerely doubted their claim. How in the world could dry, scratchy, itchy wool possibly be transformed into something that comforted dry, scratchy, itchy skin? How could something irritating become something smooth and soothing, and how could something smelly and dirty become fragrant and pure? How could thick, rough sheepskin become pure ointment? The properties are totally different. There's absolutely no resemblance between sheepskin and oil; the sheepskin would have to go through a total transformation.

I couldn't understand what the sheared wool of sheep had to do with pure oil, so I went on a mission. As I left the store, my heart was beating out of my chest. I knew the Holy Spirit wanted to show me something. I knew there was a spiritual connection.

Now, we know the most common metaphor used throughout the Bible is that of a sheep and a shepherd. The Bible calls us sheep. David identifies himself as a sheep. In Psalm 100:3 he says, "We are His people, and the sheep of His pasture" (mev). The similarities between us and sheep are uncanny. Let's look at a few sheep facts for a moment to see how well we identify with them.[1]

- Sheep Fact #1: Sheep from different flocks can be grazing together in a field, but when their shepherd calls them, they recognize the voice and go in the direction of their respective shepherds. That's what Jesus was referencing when He said in

John 10:27, "My sheep hear My voice, and I know them, and they follow Me" (mev).

- Sheep Fact #2: The sheep are kept in a pen with a narrow gate, and at night a good shepherd will lie down in front of the gate to keep predators from getting in and to keep the sheep from getting out. Sheep are gullible. They must be led or they will be easily misled. And they must stay close to the shepherd, because if they stray toward the back of the flock, the wolf can isolate them and destroy them. Jesus said in John 10:11, "I am the good shepherd. The good shepherd lays down His life for the sheep" (mev).

- Sheep Fact #3: Sheep are easily frightened and easily disturbed. They can drown in two feet of water. How easy is it for us to get fearful and frazzled? It probably doesn't take much. A letter from the IRS will cause the strongest of men to drop to his knees before he even opens the envelope! Could that be why the phrase "Do not fear" is continually repeated throughout the Bible?

- Sheep Fact #4: Encyclopedia time. Domesticated sheep produce wool, whereas wild sheep that roam from pen to pen only produce hair, which is useless. Sheep that stay under the care of one shepherd in a familiar pen, eating a steady diet, produce valuable wool. That could be why it's so important to be members of a local assembly, under the care of a shepherd, and eating a steady diet of good teaching. We will be much healthier, stronger, and more mature in the Lord if we do.

- Sheep Fact #5: The most common diseases among sheep are sore mouth and foot rot. Both are extremely contagious. Are we not brought down by the same things—saying the wrong thing, flapping our lips a little too much while influencing other sheep around us, or walking in the wrong direction and causing others to follow closely behind?

- Sheep Fact #6: All sheep must be sheared at least once a year; otherwise, the accumulation of wool will choke the lambs as they come to suck at the mother's breasts. The excess wool will block the lamb's digestive system, and it will die. In the same way, if we are not sheared from our buildup of offenses and wrong attitudes, we can cause spiritual death to a young believer.

Even though some facts about sheep are not too flattering, know this: sheep are extremely valuable. If they weren't, God would not have likened us to them. Think about the symbolism: sheep's wool is used to make coverings such as blankets, sweaters, mittens, and coats. So we too are called to be coverings for people's nakedness. We are to provide warmth for people who come to us from a cold, cruel world. Did you know that sheepskin is used in hospitals for the prevention of bedsores? So too should we bring relief to people who are hurting.

More Than Meets The Eye

Let's get back to the advertisement in the health food store. After some research, I found out that the ad was absolutely true. I discovered that what is in wool is more valuable than the wool itself! In other words, what you can't see is more valuable than what you can see. There is more than meets the eye!

Wool contains an oily substance called the yolk. The yolk is a combination of sheep's sweat and this precious, valuable ointment. Antibacterial properties are found in the ointment, and it also serves as a repellent against the heavy rains by causing the water to bead up so the wool won't become too heavy.[2]

But this valuable ointment is not only protection for the sheep; it is also provision for others. The rougher the terrain, the steeper the climb, the more the sheep sweat. The more they sweat, the more ointment they produce. So it seems that out of life's hard, everyday experiences something of value is being created. The sheep's sweat is not in vain! The shepherd wastes nothing. He literally recycles their perspiration. Somehow their burden produces a blessing for someone else.

Let's put ourselves in the sheep's place. In their matted, dirty, smelly, tangled, unsheared wool, something fragrant is being produced, but the sheep can't see it. Could it also be that, in our lives, that which is precious and the sweat of everyday life cohabit the same space? Could it be that the two commingle, as though humanity is mixed with divinity, the holy mixed with the common?

This may seem like a stretch, but the word *ointment* comes from a Latin word that is also translated *anointing*. It's as though the sheep are anointed to bring healing, but they don't have a clue.

The word *anointing* means to smear on. The sheep don't realize there is something valuable in their backbreaking load, something that can be smeared onto someone's calloused hands or dry, cracked skin. Unbeknownst to them they are carrying around the cure for the wounded, but they think they are just dumb sheep shouldering a heavy load.

On my travels in Australia I met a sheep shearer who explained that the number one mission of the shepherd is to get the sheep on the shearing table so their heavy load can be lifted and the yolk can be broken. That is how the ointment will be extracted so it can then be smeared onto someone's dry, cracked skin!

Unfortunately the number one mission of the sheep is to avoid the shearing table at all costs because they are fearful of being nicked, nipped, or bruised. They hate pain. They don't want to be undressed, uncovered, naked, or exposed. They have no idea that their momentary pain could be used for someone else's good.

If the sheep continue to avoid the shearing table, the weight of the wool will eventually cause them to tip over, and they will be unable to get up on their own. Because the shepherd knows this and the sheep's value, he boxes the sheep in until it has nowhere else to go and can do nothing except surrender.

As the load is lifted, the wool goes through an intense scouring process actually called "power washing." The wool is placed between rollers, or "put through the ringer," as I like to refer to it. It's squeezed and pressed. As the wool is untangled, the yolk is broken, and the sweat is separated from the ointment.[3] The ointment is now distributed in many different forms to heal someone else's dry, cracked skin.

Can you see the parallel between the life of the sheep and our life? Could it be that somehow mixed up in our tangled, matted mess and the sweat of our everyday burdens is the cure for someone's dry, bruised life, but we can't see it because we think we are just dumb sheep carrying a heavy load on our backs? We fail to realize that the more difficulties we go though, the more anointing and wisdom we have to share from our life experiences. We rarely think that we have sitting on the inside of us what it takes to heal someone else, but we do.

But in order for it to be shared, we have to be sheared! We have to get that heavy burden off of our backs and into the hands of the Good Shepherd. Unfortunately, just like the sheep, we avoid the shearing table at all costs. We don't want our past struggles to be uncovered, and we don't want our present struggles exposed. We just want to get by, leaving everything hidden and out of sight.

We are so afraid of what other believers will think, we become experts in dressing up our messes. We comb our matted wool, condition it, and even put pretty pink bows on it. We make excuses for it, like we're having a "bad hair day." We do everything but surrender it, because surrender is painful. We don't want our perfect exterior to be cracked. So we just keep putting spiritual outfits on our stinky, smelly life.

We dress up our messes with phrases like, "God knows my heart." Or we put on our game face when we come to church, though all the while we are suffocating under the weight of our heavy load. All the Good Shepherd wants to do is "power wash" us. He wants to lift the burden and break the "yoke" (Matt. 11:29–30) so that the anointing can be extracted and released and smeared on somebody else's open wounds!

We don't realize that our pain has the potential to be somebody else's eternal gain, that our mess has the potential to become a message of hope for the hopeless. We don't realize that anything and everything we have been through has the potential to become a life lesson for someone else. We don't realize that our greatest problem has the potential to be our greatest pulpit—that yesterday's stench is today's anointing! Didn't Paul say that *everything* that had happened to him was to advance the gospel (Phil. 1:12, 18 –22)? *The Message* puts it like this: "These things didn't shut me up; they gave me a pulpit!"

Why do you think the Bible puts everybody's "stuff" out there? The good, the bad, and the ugly is exposed and then recycled or repurposed because the anointing to minister is really in yesterday's sweat and struggle. And let me just say this: the blessing is not only in the pain we have endured, but it's also in the pain we may have caused. It's so easy for us to share our pain from a victim's standpoint, but how about sharing our own failures and the sin we have repented of while traveling on this long journey of sanctification? Aren't we all under construction? Isn't this Christian walk a growth *process*? Aren't we being made into Christ's image and likeness?

As long as we carry the burden or cover it up, it remains a burden, and when we overcome it, at best it's just a personal victory. But once we take the lid off the trash can of our past, it becomes a blessing for every other struggling saint who sits in the pew. I always say, "Let your trials pay you dividends—double for our trouble—and bring others much-needed relief." The only way for us to do that is to move just eighteen inches to victory. We must be set free from associating our failures with shame, realizing that everybody has failed on some level. Imagine what would happen in the body of Christ if we got honest with one another and stopped allowing ourselves to be trapped in a shroud of pretenses.

As Christians we have short-changed ourselves. We come to church "done" when God wants us "undone." We need to stop making ourselves look better than we really are. We need to stop being afraid of what people will think of us. When people see the real you, they'll see the real Jesus. There's a huge blessing in transparency! People are more ministered to by our weaknesses than by our perfections. Our scars tell the story that people need to hear, so we need to quit hiding them and get them out into the open.

Many years ago the Holy Spirit said these words to me: "Don't alter the altar." Altars used to be made of jagged, unhewn stone (Deut. 27:6, asv). They were put together for one primary purpose: so a sacrifice could be placed on top and lit on fire. The sacrifice was the main attraction, not the altar. But when Israel got fancy, they overlaid their altars with gold. The altars were so impressive that the sacrifice didn't seem as glorious.[4] That's what happens when we make ourselves seem better than we really are. We are polished outwardly to perfection, and the One who is the main attraction doesn't seem as impressive any longer. Even the "greats" have struggled and some have fallen, but they lived to tell about it, and their testimonies give us life.

God Uses Everything

Jesus told Peter, "Satan has asked to sift all of you as wheat. But I have prayed for you, Simon, that your faith may not fail. And when you have turned back, strengthen your brothers" (Luke 22:31–32, emphasis added). What Jesus was actually saying is: "You're going to have a blip in your faith, Petey boy. You're going to fall off the spiritual map for a few—but don't worry, Pete, I'm praying for you. I'm praying that you won't give up the fight! And when you return, which you will do, don't hide it. Push past the pain and the shame. Use your awful failure to encourage others. Allow the Holy Spirit to extract from your horrible experience something substantial to help someone else."

Maybe that's why Peter wrote in 1 Peter 5:8, "Be sober-minded; be watchful. Your adversary the devil prowls around like a roaring lion, seeking someone to devour" (esv). Peter knew that in the past he was anything but sober-minded. Instead he was filled with pride, and when you are filled with pride, you are bait for the enemy.

Look at Paul's frustration with failure and defeat. He tweets about it and Facebooks it. In Romans 7 he says (and I paraphrase), "The very things I want to do, I don't, and the things I don't want to do, I end up doing. Oh, wretched and weary man that I am! Who can save me from this body of death?" (vv. 19–24). *Really, Paul? Really? Are you kidding me?* How can you let that cat out of the bag? You, a struggling saint? Better yet—you, a flip-flopping apostle? You're an apostle who doesn't do what he wants to do and does what he doesn't want to do? *Wow!* But because Paul confesses his mess, God squeezes out a message! In Romans 8:1 Paul writes, "There is therefore now *no condemnation* for those who are in Christ Jesus" (mev, emphasis added). Paul's pain now becomes my gain. His struggle has been recycled to bring hope to my struggling life! His burden just became a blessing to my heavy heart!

But can God truly use everything, even heinous sins? Can He possibly recycle adultery, murder, an inconvenient pregnancy, the death of a child? You may be thinking, "Come on! I don't think so! How could a horrific situation give comfort and possibly minister to somebody else?" Well, David the king was dressed in royal robes, but underneath all the perfume was the stench of death after he had Bathsheba's husband killed so he could marry her himself. Few people knew what David had done, but God sent the prophet Nathan to tell the king a story about a wealthy man who stole a poor man's prized lamb (2 Sam. 12).

Just like many of us, David didn't see himself in the story until Nathan tactfully said, "You're the man. You're the man who stole a poor man's wife even though you have a harem. You're the man who had this poor, loyal man murdered to cover your tracks. Yes, David, *you* are the guilty man!" David could have made excuses. He could have said, "Well, she shouldn't have been on that rooftop taking a bath, naked, in direct view of the palace." But he didn't. He said, "Yes, I'm the man!" And once David confessed his sin, God released an anointing that would minister to others.

The key to revival is, "Confess it—don't dress it!" Immediately after David admitted that he had done wrong, Nathan said, "The Lord . . . has put away your sin" (2 Sam. 12:13, esv). Imagine that. If we are quick to confess our sin, God is quick to forgive us!

Now out of the mess we get the message. God recycled David's filthy trash and made it treasure for every fearful heart that would come after him. Psalm 32 is written out of this horrific experience. Let's read these few verses through this lens:

> Blessed is he whose transgression is forgiven, whose sin is covered. Blessed is the man against whom the Lord does not count iniquity, and in whose spirit there is no deceit. *When I kept silent, my bones wasted away* through my groaning all day long. For day and night Your hand was heavy upon me; my strength was changed into the drought of summer. Selah. *I acknowledged my sin to You, and my iniquity I did not conceal. I said, "I will confess my transgressions to the Lord,"* and You forgave the iniquity of my sin. Selah.
> —Psalm 32:1–5, mev, emphasis added

I used to read those verses as though a mean, judgmental God was pointing His finger at David, saying, "*You are the man*, you filthy good-for-nothing!" But it was really God saying, "David, you are the man. As long as you keep silent, your anointing cannot flow. I miss those songs you used to write to Me. I miss My time with you. Please don't avoid Me any longer. Let Me shear the guilt off your back so it can be smeared onto someone else's pain and guilt. Just give it to Me and watch what I can do with it."

Do you get it? The mouth that got Peter into trouble was the same mouth, now recycled, that preached some of the greatest, most effective sermons ever. Paul, the self-righteous, legalistic murderer who once produced nothing but death, now recycled becomes the greatest messenger of God's grace and freedom.

And how about Naomi? She said, "Don't call me Naomi. Call me Mara, bitter, for God has dealt harshly with me." (See Ruth 1:20.) As I read those words, the Holy Spirit shouted on the inside of my spirit, "No,

Naomi, don't call yourself bitter. I've preserved your life for a purpose. You don't know this, My precious daughter, but your God can make fine wine out of sour grapes. He gives the oil of gladness in exchange for the spirit of heaviness." The wisdom Naomi didn't have for herself she had for Ruth, because someway, somehow, she surrendered her bitterness and grief. Naomi allowed the Holy Spirit to power wash her, and thus the yoke was broken and the anointing was released.

We know from Naomi's past that when there was a famine of sorts, her tendency was to run. But this time she encouraged Ruth to go to Boaz's field and to glean from there. Little did Naomi know, by not reacting the way she had reacted in the past she changed not only the trajectory of her life but also the course of history.

When Naomi encouraged Ruth to glean in Boaz's field, she didn't have a clue that her Moabite daughter-in-law would one day very soon give birth to a baby who would be in the bloodline of Jesus. She didn't know that as she exhorted Ruth not to run because she knew that God would provide, her great-greatgrandson would be a psalmist, a giant killer, and a man after God's own heart. Had she not been sheared, her anointing would have remained all locked up, confined in her disappointment and pain, and she wouldn't have been able to share hope with Ruth. The story starts off with a famine, but it ends with a crop of righteousness that is still being produced to this day!

Charles Spurgeon said, "Why do we dread the clouds that darken our sky? It is true that for a while the dark clouds hide the sun, but it is not extinguished and it will soon shine again. Meanwhile those clouds are filled with rain, and the darker they are, the more likely they are to bring plentiful showers. How can we have rain without clouds? Our troubles have always brought us blessings, and they always will, for they are the dark chariots of God's bright and glorious grace. Before long the clouds will be emptied, and every tender plant will be happier due to the showers."[5]

It has been said that A.W. Tozer often felt like a miserable failure,[6] and Andrew Bonar said he often felt deep regret.[7] We are all the same on the inside. Just as the anointing oil was a combination of bitter and sweet, spices for living and spices for burial, so it is with us. Our anointing comes from our victories as well as our defeats. Our mess is someone else's medicine.

I'm so glad those great men of old wrote about their struggles and fears. I'm so glad they penned about their weaknesses. Those are the very things that have given people like me hope. I love to hear of others' successes, but those victories don't empower me the same way the story of a fallen man—one who was down and out—who got up and made it to the finish line because God wasn't quite finished with him.

Look at how the Lord redirected, repurposed, recycled, and transformed so many different kinds of people and circumstances. This speaks to the fact that there is nothing, absolutely nothing—not a thing!—that the Master cannot redeem for His glory! The Lord never counts anyone out. The only one who could count you out is you!

Allow me to end with this story. I had the opportunity to minister at Angola State Prison in Louisiana. I shared this illustration about the sheep's wool and pure oil, and after the meeting a prisoner stood waiting to see me. When I came to where he was, he handed me a small guitar. He proceeded to tell me that he made it out of ravaged wood left after Hurricane Katrina. He said he gathered all the broken pieces, smoothed out the rough edges, sanded them down, and glued them together. He polished it, sealed it, and put strings on it, and now it's a beautiful instrument, crafted perfectly to make music to the Lord.

That's what God does with our lives. He gathers *all* the broken pieces, puts us back together, smooths out the rough edges, and polishes us up so our lives can become a beautiful melody that can give Him glory. Our lives become instruments of praise. But we have to place the broken pieces into the hands that can craft us into something beautiful. I'm sure if all those broken pieces in our lives could speak, they would say, "This is the end of the road for me. There is no way at this stage of the game I could ever be transformed or recycled into something of purpose." But only God knows the immense potential lying dormant in every life. It is never the end of the road once something is placed into the hands of the Master who knows how to re-create masterpieces. It's just the end of that particular road.

Can you imagine what I would have thought if the man at Angola prison had handed me the polished instrument without telling me where the wood came from? Imagine if I didn't know about the violent storm that had swept through and all that the wood had endured. Imagine if I didn't know the history behind the creation of this instrument. Had I not known all of those things, I would have thought the guitar was just a beautiful instrument made from perfect wood taken from a perfect tree planted in a perfectly climate-controlled forest. It wouldn't have had any real significant meaning to me. I probably would have been more impressed with the instrument than with the one who saw what a damaged, water-stained piece of wood could become.

That's exactly how it is when we allow people to admire who we are without telling them where we came from. That's what happens when we fail to tell people that sin had torn our lives apart, but there was a merciful God who saw us as polished long before we were anything remotely close to what He has caused us to become. Oh, what a disservice we do to the name of our God and to those we are witnessing to. It's in sharing those personal and sometimes painful things that hope is birthed for all.

Oh, make no mistake about it, we do have quite a story to tell once we have the courage to be honest and share it. I know what it's like to feel like a piece of trash, but I also know what it means to be recycled, repurposed, and transformed by the grace of God. Because of where I've been, I know how others feel, and because of that I can see their untapped potential. It would be quite a shame if I was satisfied with what God has done for me and just kept the story of how He changed my life all locked up inside.

We are salve for the weary, balm for the broken, dressing for the burned, and medicine for this sin-sick world. So let's allow the Holy Spirit to lift our burden and break the yoke so what's valuable can be extracted. It's definitely already inside of us. We're a mere eighteen inches from victory if we would just allow the Holy Spirit to use our past. As 1 John 2:27 says, *as for you, you've been given an anointing, which you received from Him, and it resides permanently in you.*

Let's Pray

Precious Holy Spirit, please open my eyes to see that my past trash can become someone else's treasure today as I share with them in total honesty what You can do with a life no matter how stinky it is at the present time. Give me the courage to share the good, the bad, and the ugly, and allow me to tell others how You recycled all my fears, insecurities, and failures. Lord, allow Your work of grace to continue through my testimony, in Jesus's name, amen.

Maria Durso

CHAPTER 10 – ALL ACCESS

Not long ago my husband and I were invited to attend a conference held at a megachurch. The keynote speakers were some of the top preachers and teachers of the day, and the who's who of Christian leaders were in attendance. We were invited as guests because our son Chris was speaking about youth and young adult ministry at one of the breakout sessions.

When we arrived at the gorgeous hotel where we were staying, there was an escort waiting for us. He introduced himself and said he would be our driver to and from the conference. He also said he was available to help us with "whatever" we needed, including Starbucks. He said, "Tell me what you want and how you want it, day or night. I'll be stationed here to meet your every need."

When we left him, we went up to our room to drop off our luggage, and waiting for us was an over-the-top gift basket. It was filled with exotic waters with names I'd never heard before, unusual snacks that I'd never seen before, and fruit that must have been delivered from the Promised Land—there were humongous grapes and pears. When I got to the bottom of the magnificent basket, I noticed there were beautifully wrapped boxes with our names on them. They were gifts, handpicked and tailor-made for my husband and me. *Wow!* And to top it all off (as if that were not enough), there was an invitation to the home of this famous pastor whose church was hosting the conference! Sweat was now dripping from my arched brow!

We left the beautiful basket and went back down to the lobby to proceed to the conference. Just as promised, our escort was waiting for us, ready to shuttle us where we needed to go. When we walked over to him, he handed us a bag, a bracelet, and a badge with the words "All Access." He said those items would give us all access into the greenroom, where the guest speakers would eat and rest throughout the day. He said everything would be *free*. "You never have to leave the grounds," he added. Then he informed us that we had seats reserved for us near the front of the massive auditorium.

I was feeling a bit overwhelmed and a bit uncomfortable, even fearful. I felt like I was totally out of my league, like I didn't belong. I'm from New York, and this church's kindness was making me nervous. What could they possibly want from us, and why were they being so kind? So needless to say, we didn't sit in the reserved seats. We sat near the back in the lower mezzanine. We never went into the greenroom, though we did sneak a peek or two of the inside. We basically stayed on the outside of the room, around the perimeter, and watched the other guests as they went inside.

Along with our All Access passes we were given a key. This was for use in the hotel, and it was the key to *free*. The key was to the concierge luxury suite, so it gave us access to free breakfast, snacks, and hors d'oeuvres in the evening. The room was filled with *free* amenities, but we didn't know it! Our son knew it! He and his wife were eating up a storm. He thought we knew about it, but sadly enough we didn't. We were paying for our meals.

We held in our possession the bag, the bracelet, and the badge, but because we felt we didn't "earn" any of these privileges, we didn't think we deserved them. Then something suddenly dawned on me, and I got this profound revelation: we were basically getting this royal treatment because of our son! We didn't have all access because of anything we did; it was because of the "son connection" that we were given reserved seats, lovely gifts, greenroom privileges, and a personal invitation to the pastor's home.

All my years in ministry didn't get me to that particular place; the "son connection" alone opened that door. It's just like the connection we have to Jesus. God's Son gives us privileges we could have never earned—free daily bread, day or night; gifts that are tailor-made for us; an open invitation into the Most Holy Place; and reserved seats right up close and personal in the throne room!

On the last day of the conference, the escort said to us, "They really want you to sit up front in the reserved seats they have for you." My husband and I reluctantly agreed, and like death-row inmates walking to our execution, we walked down the *long* aisle to the seats they had reserved for us. When we got to our place, I not only saw that the seats had our names on them but I also realized that they had remained empty all those days. As I went to sit down, the woman in the seat next to mine jumped to her feet and shouted, "Maria Durso, where have you been? I've been waiting for you. Come and take your seat!"

I felt like the Holy Spirit was causing the woman's words to reverberate in the very depths of my being: *Maria, where have you been? I've been waiting for you. Come and take your seat!* Here I was wearing the badge and the bracelet, and holding the bag, yet I wasn't taking advantage of the access those items gave me. Right there I clearly saw such a similarity to God's people. We have our Bibles, our bumper stickers, and our buildings, but few people realize that "all access" really means *all access*! We don't believe that *I* or "someone like me" really has the right to such lofty privileges!

I said, "Lord, what is wrong with me? Why am I so sheepish when it comes to receiving Your blessings?" The Bible says in Psalm 119:130, "The giving of Your words gives light" (mev). God's Word was going to give me a brain wash.

No Limits

All access: no limits, no restrictions.
Access: the act of bringing to, a moving to; access, approach.[1]

The Bible tells us that as new covenant believers we all have all access. We all have access into the concierge level of heaven. Ephesians 2:18 says, "For through Him we . . . have access by one Spirit to the Father" (mev). We *all* have reserved seats in heaven's most sacred place. The term *new covenant* simply means "new arrangement." A new arrangement has been made to get us into a place we would never have been allowed to go.

In the Old Testament the common man was absolutely *not* allowed to enter the holy places of the tabernacle. Outside, yes; inside, no! The common man wasn't from the right family, the right tribe, the right sect, or the right bloodline. He wasn't the "right kind." He was born on the wrong side of the tracks, so to speak. He was considered unworthy. If I lived in those days, my badge would certainly read, "No Access."

The high priest alone went behind the veil. The veil was a thick curtain—a massive, imposing wall of separation sixty feet high and thirty feet wide. Jewish historians say it took three hundred priests to move it. Man, I wouldn't want to be around during spring cleaning when they had to take it down, clean it, and hang it back up!

The message God obviously wanted to send was that there were places in the tabernacle that were "off limits." If there were signs hanging around those areas of the temple, they would read, "Keep Out! No Trespassing." The high priest alone had the "All Access" pass. He alone had access to the concierge, gold, and penthouse levels.

But even he had restrictions! He could use his "All Access" pass only one time per year on the Day of Atonement. It wasn't "All Access" all the time! If the priest wasn't right before God, he would fall dead behind that massive curtain, and someone would have to take a long staff to pull him out from underneath it. So as much as being a high priest was a privilege, the position probably brought with it a lot of fear, dread, anxiety, and even panic.

Let's put ourselves in this poor priest's shaking sandals. Can you imagine what this poor man went through the night before he was to go into the holy of holies? He was probably thinking, "Did I dot all my i's and cross all my t's? Did I read *all* of the law to my son? Did I take out the garbage? Was I good to my mother-in-law? Is today my last on earth?" *Oy vey!*

There was torment attached to the position, because if the priest made a mistake, he could end up dead! But here comes the New Testament. In Matthew 27:51 the Bible declares that when Jesus gave up His Spirit, simultaneously miles away in the temple, the massive veil, the imposing wall of separation, was torn from top to bottom. It was as though invisible hands reached out and ripped the curtain into shreds. Heaven was obviously sending a new message. Now "whoever believes" can go inside (John 3:16). Someone else paid our debt. Someone else was holy in our stead. There is now an open door giving us access.

When the veil tore, the mercy seat was exposed, and now there is an open door of communication between us and God, an open door to receive revelation. Now we can live in the presence of God. Now we *all* can hear the voice of God. So Jesus's death and that ripped veil ended the elite system of only a few, one time per year, going before the Lord in the most holy place. No more haves and have-nots, Jew and Gentile, slave and free. Red and yellow, black and white, we are all precious in His sight. No longer was it about our bloodline; it became all about His blood.

Under the new arrangement the minister and the laymen *all* have all access *all the time*. Not only are we invited in, but we are also entreated to come inside as often as we want, and we are encouraged to come inside with boldness (Heb. 4:16). That's the posture God wants us to have. He tells us, "Don't come inside tiptoeing around fearfully and sheepishly." He tells us to come inside like we belong inside. We are His children. He's saying, "Come on in! I took away the veil. No more locked-off places. The door is open. *Come inside.* I'm waiting!"

Listen, we who are evil know how to give good gifts to our children. (See Matthew 7:11.) We parents don't expect our kids to come over to our house fearfully. We expect them to just come over. They don't have to bring us flowers or a piece of cake. They are not guests; they are our children. My kids are married, and they come over whenever they want. We could be in our pajamas resting with the door locked, but that doesn't stop them. My little grandchildren know where we hide the key. Nothing stops them from coming inside and climbing into bed with us. They know that they have all access *all the time* to any room in the house. They also know that they are always welcome. If they ever came in fearfully, I would feel hurt and insulted. I would feel like they didn't know I always want to see them!

Boldness: free and fearless confidence, cheerful courage, assurance.[2]

You and I won't ever have to worry about dropping dead or being turned away from God, because the basis of our boldness is the blood of Jesus. Hebrews 10:22 says, "Let us draw near to God with a sincere heart and with the full assurance that faith brings, having our hearts sprinkled to cleanse us from a guilty conscience and having our bodies washed with pure water." The only reason you and I are allowed to draw near to God with boldness is the blood of Jesus. It's nothing except the blood. No longer outsiders, we're insiders, behind-the-curtain insiders—all access, red carpet, greenroom, concierge-level insiders!

Leviticus 17:11 says, "The life of the flesh is in the blood" (mev). Well, the spiritual life of the believer is faith in the precious blood of Jesus! If it's nothing but the blood that washed away my sin, then it's nothing but the blood. It it's nothing but the blood that makes me whole again, then it's nothing but the blood—not my performance! No other fount I know makes me white as snow. The only payment for our debt that heaven recognizes is the blood! It cleanses us; it redeems us; it justifies us; it qualifies us.

In Exodus 12:21–29 God instructed the Israelites to place the blood of a spotless lamb across their doorposts. Then and only then would the death angel pass over and those inside the house would live. We can't hang our tithing envelopes or our hours of service in the house of the Lord across the "doorposts" of our lives and receive new life. All those things are good, but they can never replace the blood of Jesus.

Leviticus 1 gives instructions for how sinners should bring their sin offering to the priest. There was one major requirement: the lamb had to be sinless. When he stood in front of the priest who served as judge and jury, the sinner had to place his hand on the lamb's forehead. As he did, immediately the sinner's sins were imputed onto that spotless lamb, and the innocence of the lamb was transferred onto him. That is what we know as the doctrine of substitution. The lamb took the sinner's place—period.

The priest never put the sinner under a magnifying glass and inspected him thoroughly. He also never checked to see if there were marks in his Torah to make sure he was doing his daily devotionals, or calluses on his knees to make sure he spent ample time praying. He didn't watch to make sure his church attendance was up to par. The only thing the priest inspected was the lamb. So it is with us. If we should by chance slip, fall, or stumble into sin, God looks at the spotless Lamb as our substitute. Our life is hidden in Christ. When the Father sees us, He sees Jesus. It's as though we've been Photoshopped and all the wrinkles have been removed. That's how God sees at us. It's us minus the flaws.

Because of the blood we have confidence. The word *confidence* is used thirty-one times in the New Testament. The word means firm and unshakable. It indicates a sense of complete freedom— freedom that comes from an intimate relationship with God and full assurance of our acceptance by Him. Hebrews 10:20 tells us that the curtain opened a new and living way. This way is refreshing and life-giving, not filled with death, condemnation, and dread. Jesus is the source of life, not death. To accept this there has to be a paradigm shift in the very core of our being; otherwise, we will live as the Old Testament priests did—under the law of fear and dread each and every time we approach the throne. That is why the

Bible warns us in Hebrews 10:35, "Do not throw away your confidence." It also says in 1 John 3:21, "Beloved, if our heart does not condemn us, we have confidence toward God" (nkjv).

We all sin. The word *sin* simply means to miss the mark. We *all* have fallen short and most likely are an inch or two off the mark every day in some way, shape, or form. So when we do sin, God doesn't want us to go through mental gymnastics. He doesn't want us to figure out a plan to get back into God's good graces. *Just confess it; don't dress it!* The word *confess* doesn't mean to beg, plead, or live in misery. It simply means to agree with God concerning our sin. Sin doesn't cause us to lose our position with God, but it does block our fellowship with Him. It's just like in the parable of the prodigal son: the prodigal never stopped being a son, but because he went far away, he lost fellowship, communication, and even his privileges as a son.

In the story of the prodigal son in Luke 15:11–32, you'll notice his father never moved from his position as the prodigal's father. While the prodigal was a very long way off, he remembered his father's house, and as soon as he did, the son started going through all these mental gymnastics. He said: "I know. I'll go back and tell my father that I no longer deserve to be called his son. Let me see . . . how should I go back? I know what I'll do. I'll go . . . um . . . back . . . as a servant!" But while he was running toward the house, the father came out and ran toward him. The father didn't want a speech; he just wanted his son!

Fellowship was immediately restored—no questions asked; just a father's strong embrace! He didn't care about the son's stench; he didn't care that he broke the law and touched pigs; he didn't care that he squandered all of his inheritance. All he cared about was that his son was now home, and as long as he had food, clothes, and shelter, his son would have a place to go, something to eat, and clothes to wear.

There were no limits, no boundaries to the amount of grace that father had to give his son. *Wow!* That's just like the incredible extravagance of God's grace. When we sin, all we have to say is, "I'm so sorry, my Lord. Please forgive me. I agree with You. I confess that I have missed the mark, but I also agree that Your blood has been shed to cleanse me and make me whiter than snow." The more we understand the magnificent, amazing grace of God, the quicker, the greater, and the more magnanimous our confession will be. We won't wrap our confession in blame and fancy excuses. We will be ever so grateful that the One who knows us the best wants to quickly relieve us of anything that would cause a breach in our relationship. In Philippians 3:3 we are exhorted to place no confidence in the flesh.

Why The Conflict?

So let's be honest, why the struggle? Why the internal conflict? Why the raging war? What is at the root of this conflict? What is the enemy of our confidence?

The enemy of our confidence is our conscience! Our conscience is in conflict with our confidence. What exactly is our conscience? Our conscience is our innermost soul and consciousness. It's our moral barometer. It's where we get our moral sensitivity or scruples. This was put in us by God to show us right from wrong, and it works in conjunction with the law. But who can keep the law?

Romans 7:14 says, "We know that the law is spiritual, but I am carnal, sold under sin" (mev). He's saying, "I just can't keep the law." Realize this: if we break just one part of the law, we have broken the whole law! Our conscience, which was put in us by God, is what drove us to God. The problem with our conscience is that the very thing that convicts us accuses us. It *never* shuts off! It isn't wired to receive forgiveness. It's just like the law; it's black and white. It can't be satisfied.

Just as the tablets Moses held on Mount Sinai were made of weighty, cold, hard stone, so our guilty conscience and accusing memory are weights that can seem too heavy to bear. Our conscience is our prosecutor, whereas our confidence is our advocate. My conscience keeps me conscious of *all* my flaws and weaknesses and reminds me why I don't "deserve" to have a relationship with God and why I shouldn't be running into His presence with boldness and confidence! My conscience doesn't want me to fix my thoughts on Jesus (Heb. 12:2). It wants me to fix my thoughts on me, "the big mess up." Confidence, on the other hand, keeps me conscious of who He is and who He will cause me to become!

Hebrews 9:9 tells us that all the gifts and sacrifices being offered under the old covenant weren't enough to clear the conscience of the worshipper. Notice the Bible declares it was the conscience of the worshippers that needed to be cleared. It doesn't say that all the sacrifices were unable to clear the sin from the sinner. No! The sin was pardoned once the lamb was slain. Those rituals were not able to clear the *conscience* of the worshipper.

Imagine the worshipper, the God-lover, the one who wanted to live right and please God. It wouldn't matter if he brought a thousand unblemished lambs; his conscience never let him off the hook. He could never be delivered of his "consciousness" of sin. He knew theoretically, according to the Book of Leviticus, that the shedding of the blood of a lamb put him in right standing, but *in his heart* he was always conscious that he was a sinner. He never felt clean. He felt like he didn't deserve to be forgiven.

This is precisely why God scrapped the old system and made a new arrangement. This was the root problem with the old covenant. It was a "broken system" on the worshippers' end, not on God's end! Hebrews 7:18–19 says, "For there is then an annulling of the previous commandment due to its weakness and uselessness. For the law made nothing perfect, but now a better hope is introduced, by which we draw near to God" (mev). And we read in Hebrews 8:7–8, "For if there had been nothing wrong with that first covenant, no place would have been sought for another. But God found fault with the people."

Don't you see? The worshipper was unable to ever feel clean! Hebrews 10:2–3 tells us that the repeated sacrifices were just a reminder of the people's sins. Instead of feeling clean, they just felt guiltier. If those sacrifices could have stopped the guilt—the bleeding, the hemorrhaging of defeat and discouragement—then God wouldn't have stopped the ritual. But in order to stop the bleeding of the conscience, our Savior, the perfect Lamb, had to shed His blood!

C. S. Lewis describes Satan's strategy so eloquently in *The Screwtape Letters*: get Christians preoccupied with their failures, and from then on the battle is won. Hebrews 10:21–22 says, "Since [which means it's a done deal] we have a great High Priest . . . let us *go right into the presence of God* with *sincere hearts* fully trusting him. For our [evil or] guilty consciences have been sprinkled with Christ's blood to make us clean" (nlt, emphasis added). In this context an evil or guilty conscience is found in someone who is always under sin's accusation or in someone who is always sinning!

An evil or guilty conscience always accuses the finished work of Christ. It whispers, "What Christ did is good but not quite good enough to allow someone like you into His presence freely, with no strings attached!" It says, "There has to be a catch!" The voice of a guilty conscience is oppressive and keeps us in bondage. It creates a self-imposed prison that keeps us insecure. An evil conscience is a confidence killer. It's a bully that beats us up every day. It's my inner critic, my personal scorekeeper. It constantly drags me back to the scene of the crime. It causes me to feel self-loathing and shame. My evil conscience tells me that I'm not good enough—I'm not God's choice servant. I'm not USDA approved. I'm not the right kind. He's never quite satisfied with me.

A guilty conscience doesn't allow God to love all the mess out of me because I feel I have to get all the mess out of myself in order for Him to love me! It causes me to see God like one of the judges on the Food Network show *Chopped*. On the show four chefs get baskets filled with crazy ingredients that are odd and often would never normally be prepared together. The chefs have to figure out what the ingredients are exactly and how to prepare them in a way that will make them succulent. This has to be done in fifteen to thirty minutes, depending on the round. Oh, let me not forget, the presentation is also a factor. In each round—appetizer, main course, and dessert—one chef is "chopped." There's too much salt, or it's not tasty enough, too soggy, not cooked enough, or cooked too much. Whatever the reason, they're told, "You've been chopped!"

Well, sometimes life seems exactly like that show. We are handed a basket with ingredients that don't make any sense. We feel we have to figure out the solutions to our complicated messes in record time, all on our own. Feeling overwhelmed, we usually overcompensate, or we don't do enough. We check out or lose our tempers, usually feeling that our behavior as God's children is less than acceptable. We sense a voice deep down inside us say, "You've been chopped!" And thinking it's the voice of God, we end up feeling like "basket cases"! We walk away feeling like we never make the cut!

But here's the good news: Hebrews 9:14 says, "How much more shall the blood of Christ . . . cleanse your conscience from dead works to serve the living God?" (mev). What are those futile, feeble acts that lead to spiritual death? It's being on the never-ending, vicious treadmill of guilt and self-loathing that goes nowhere. It's straining at the oars to be good enough. It's having good intentions with bad results. When we live a life of trying to gain God's approval day in and day out, then we are no different from those Old Testament priests.

When Jesus was on the cross, He said, "It is finished" (John 19:30, mev), then He later sat down at the right hand of the Father (Mark 16:19) and now intercedes for you and me (Rom. 8:34). He's praying that we get on with our relationship with Him without fear and dread! The blood of Jesus puts an end to all our fruitless deeds so we can hurry up and get into the throne room and have a real relationship with our God. That's all He ever wanted from the moment He made mankind—He wanted someone He could pour Himself into and love!

The debt we once owed can never be paid back, and God doesn't expect us to repay it. So it stands to reason that it must be paid forward. The only outstanding debt that we owe is to love one another (Rom. 13:8). That's it! That's all we are expected to pay back. We are just to pay God's love forward! Going forward is where all the action is—living in total freedom, debt-free! We must live to give out the same mercy we've been given! We are to love with the same measure with which we have been loved. I know that's the only thing that will please the heart of God!

The apostle Paul tells Timothy, his son in the faith, "The only way you can fight the good fight of faith is by holding on to faith and a good conscience!" (1 Tim. 1:18 –19, my paraphrase). That's the dynamic duo. That's the one-two punch! Paul is warning Timothy that there's no other way to be victorious through the treacherous battle day in and day out. He had to *hold on* to faith and a good conscience.

The same is true for you. Don't ever let go of these two vital ingredients:

1. Faith—in the finished work of Jesus Christ, not faith in faith or faith in your good works.
2. A good conscience—the knowledge that you are in right standing with God because of the blood of Jesus. We must put our conscience in line with God's Word. If the Word says God is satisfied and the debt has been paid, then we must by faith speak the Word of God to our accusing conscience. If the conscience knows that God is satisfied, then our conscience will be satisfied.

The revelation of this word brings about a revolution. This is revolutionary thinking that must transpire eighteen inches deep down in our innermost being. Revelation 12:10–11 says, "For the accuser of our brethren . . . has been cast down. And they overcome him by the blood of the Lamb and by the word of their testimony" (nkjv). This is the bottom line. The blood of Jesus ends all conversation with our conscience as we declare that the blood has given us "All Access"!

The blood sealed the deal! We're not dead men walking, but we've been made alive forevermore! Let's take an eighteen-inch victory walk. Let's leave the path of guilt and shame, and walk eighteen inches onto the path of freedom and liberty!

Just like the woman at the conference said to me, so I believe the Holy Spirit is saying to you as you are reading these words: "(Insert your name right now), where have you been? I've been waiting for you. Come and take your seat!" No one else can ever take your seat! It has your name on it. It will remain empty because no one else can take your place! God has given you a personal invitation into His house. There are gifts tailor-made just for you. There's a room filled with free food for you to feast on—there's bread of life from the table of the Lord.

We also have been given a personal escort. He is the Holy Spirit, the One who leads us and guides us into *all* truth!

We don't need the bag, the bracelet, or the badge because we have *the blood!* From now on, let's move to a new address. No more living on Pitiful Place, Depression Drive, or Oppression Overpass. Let's live on Confidence Court, Approval Avenue, Love Lane, and Boldness Boulevard because we *all* have *all access!* This is the good news of the gospel of Jesus Christ! *Hallelujah!*

Let's Pray

Father, thank You for sending Jesus in my place. Thank You, Jesus, for shedding Your precious blood for all sins—the ones I've committed and the ones I will commit. I will never trample underfoot the Son of God or insult the Spirit of Grace by knowingly and callously sinning. Nor will I insult You any longer by not accepting the finished work of the cross, because I now understand that when You said, "It is finished," You meant exactly that. I will never try to add anything else to what You have done except to pay forward the mercy You have freely given me by Your grace. In Jesus's name, amen.

CHAPTER 11 – GETTING TO THE ROOT OF DEPRESSION

The Bible tells us is in Proverbs 12:25, "Anxiety in the heart . . . causes depression" (nkjv). When we think of depression, we naturally think of an illness of the mind, which is definitely true in the medical sense. I realize that there are definite chemical imbalances in the brain that can cause extreme mood swings. We as ladies know about imbalances when it is that time of the month and our hormones are totally out of whack. Clearly this verse in Proverbs is not addressing depression caused by a chemical or hormonal medical condition. I believe it is clearly speaking about being overwhelmed by life's circumstances and the curveballs that come our way. I believe it is speaking about something that is rarely addressed: *spiritual depression*!

Almost every person we read about in God's Word has suffered from this malady in one way, shape, or form, and it is unfortunately still affecting many of God's people today. Many people, whether saved or unsaved, are convinced in their hearts and minds that they have been abandoned by God. They fear that either God doesn't see their situation or that He does see but doesn't care. When it comes to fear, worry, and anxiety, I don't think there are areas that are off limits. I believe both the head and the heart are involved. I believe the worries of life that might start in the head oftentimes find a home in the heart.

The apostle Paul strongly exhorts us in Philippians 4:6–7, "Be anxious for nothing [nothing means nothing], but in *everything*, by prayer and supplication with gratitude, make your requests known to God. And the peace of God, which surpasses all understanding, will protect your *hearts and minds* through Christ Jesus" (mev, emphasis added). Clearly we see here that nursing anxious thoughts infiltrates both the head and the heart. Paul prays for God to guard them both, because once anxiety is allowed to take root, depression is sure to follow.

Doesn't it stand to reason that bouts of depression could occur when the heart is on overload? Proverbs 12:25 seems to zero in on the heart as the base where anxiety seems to rest its ugly head and then spreads out and weaves itself into the fabric of our daily lives. Could it be that when the brain of the heart is bogged down with many anxious thoughts, our moods and our outlook on life and God are affected? David said of his heart in Psalm 61:2, "When *my heart* faints, lead me to the rock that is higher than I" (mev, emphasis added).

Notice that David didn't say "if" my heart is overwhelmed. No, he said "when" my heart is overwhelmed, which means circumstances in life will happen that *will* overwhelm us. Also, he said when "my heart" is overwhelmed, not when "my mind" is overwhelmed! Obviously David suffered from bouts of depression "in his heart," and he needed to be taken to a place that was far past the eighteen inches to his mind.

David knew it would take far more than positive thinking (though there is nothing wrong with thinking positively) to unravel the darkness that was pulling him into the oblivion of spiritual depression. David knew it would take the divine hand of God to pull him up from the gravitational pull that would try to take him down. He knew that only the light of God could come and pierce the darkness and give him faith to go on.

The Bible clearly states that David felt *his heart* was being gripped by damaging thoughts that were overpowering him, and we can clearly see why. From the moment Samuel anointed David the next king, the brain in David's heart had many opportunities to be weighed down. It had many opportunities to collect negative data. David wasn't even a consideration when Samuel came to anoint one of Jesse's sons to be king over Israel. He was just an afterthought, like, "Oh, yeah, him. We forgot about him."

I know many of us can relate to that kind of attitude. I remember when my husband and I were asked to pastor the first church to be planted out of the Brooklyn Tabernacle. Many people came up to us and said, "*You*? Really? *You and Michael*?" In other words, they were saying, "Couldn't they find anyone better than you?" They didn't vocalize these next words, but their expressions and body languages spoke loud and clear: "You guys aren't 'minister material.' You guys aren't trained. You don't come from good Christian stock. Your family tree isn't connected to previous generations of Christians who have left their mark on this world." In other words, "You are 'nobodies'!"

Those words, even the ones that were technically unspoken, went deep into the very fabric of my being, and I felt for years that somehow Pastor Cymbala and his elders must have made a grave error. We weren't polished, nor were we scholars by any means. Even now as I type this page, I remember writing something to someone, pouring out my heart. The person never commented on what I wrote, only on my grammatical errors. The person said it was annoying when people used an excessive number of commas, and shut me down for decades. Here I am decades later, climbing up from a spiritual depression of sorts and giving writing another shot!

Some commentators have said that David was illegitimate because there is no record of his mother's name in his genealogy. Imagine having *all* those brothers from the same mother and father, but your mom is nowhere to be found. David was just the "nobody" of the family who was left to guard the flocks. He was the "nobody" who was left on his own to kill bears and lions to protect the family's investment. Did David also think he was a "nobody" in the eyes of God?

Well, the "nobody" stepped up to kill the taunting giant, Goliath, but in the midst of such an extraordinary act he was looked down upon by King Saul because he didn't have the proper armor. Then he was mocked by Goliath because his weapon was meager, to say the least. The nobody killed the giant and married Saul's daughter as a reward, only to have her ripped away from him and given to another man (2 Sam. 3:13–16).

And the list goes on and on. He was chased by King Saul, the jealous madman, for approximately ten years, and there were many scandals in David's family. David's son Amnon raped his half-sister Tamar. Then Tamar's brother Absalom killed Amnon to avenge his sister's rape. Later on Absalom tried *to* tear his father David's kingdom away from him by causing division. David couldn't have been more on point than when he penned the famous words in Psalm 23, "Even though I walk through the valley of the shadow of death, I will fear no evil; for You are with me" (v. 4, mev).

Valleys are enclosed and dark and can get a bit chilly. Those types of dark spiritual valleys came often for David. The good times always seemed to be overshadowed by an arrow of discouragement tailor-made to pierce deep into his heart. That is how life is for many believers. Many consecrated believers are well acquainted with the valley low. They know all too well the dark times that seem so dreadful and how they seem to hide the light of God's presence. Some experience valleys that are so deep they can't see a way out. Isn't this what the great saints of old called "the dark night of the soul"?

Hope In God!

Depression in the heart! What angst David must have lived with, yet he kept looking to the Lord . . . or, should I say, he made himself look to the Lord. In Psalm 42:5 an incident is recorded in which David would speak to his soul and ask why—why are you so downcast? Oh, David knew exactly "why" as he watched his life play out like a bad movie. Yet through it all he continually commanded his soul to "hope in God."

We clearly see throughout the Psalms that this was the strategy David used in dealing with overwhelming thoughts of despair. He kept the eyes of his heart fixed, stayed, focused, pinned on the Lord. He did what Hebrews 12:2 commands us to do long before the words were ever penned. Although his circumstances pointed to the valley, his heart lived on another plane! David the trained warrior knew that if the eyes of his heart strayed, then darkness would win, and that wasn't even an option for him. David refused to live life in the valley when he knew the target he was aiming at was eighteen inches above him.

Every time that he would state his case to the Lord and tell Him his tale of woe as he was sliding deeper into despair, he would somehow look up as though he had rocket fuel underneath him. He would begin the psalm recounting his sorrows and remembering his enemies, and then end it by recalling the goodness of God. Isn't that what keeps us going through the dark times? But could it really be that simple? How can we possibly look up when our hearts are weighed down with despair?

David was such a disciplined young man. He did what the Bible tells us to do in 2 Corinthians 10:5: he took hold of every thought and made it subject to the authority of God. Just as he wrestled the bear and the lion, he aggressively wrestled those thoughts that he clearly knew were his enemy. He knew those thoughts had come to rip him into shreds and destroy his life. And so he pounded them down until they had no more breath. He used the same tactics of warfare in the spiritual valley that he had used in the valley as he tended the sheep. He knew that when depressing thoughts entered his heart, he became the sheep that needed to be saved. And what can save us from the snare of negative thinking except the power of the Word of God?

The Bible says God's Word is living and active (Heb. 4:12). That means it's alive and has energy. It has movement. It's a weapon unto itself. Every written word on the page becomes alive as we receive it inside our hearts. It then becomes our fuel and rips to shreds the thoughts that want to rip us asunder.

In Psalm 27:3 David states, "Though an army should encamp against me, *my heart will not fear*" (mev, emphasis added). Then toward the end of this psalm, in verse 13, he says, "I believe I will see the goodness of the Lord in the land of the living" (mev). So time and time again, as David saw the enemy of negative thinking trying to take its place in the deepest recesses of his heart and make itself a permanent resident, he strategically disciplined himself to direct the thoughts of his heart toward the Lord and His Word. By thinking about God's Word—by hiding God's Word in his heart—David was able to see the power of God's Word expel the darkness! Light always overcomes darkness! So without David even being aware of the scientific research, he was actually making the brain of his heart meditate on the goodness of God and His past faithfulness.

We too can discipline ourselves to receive God's Word to overcome negative thoughts. It's cardio for the brain of the heart. It's working the brain's muscle to become stronger instead of fainting at the first sign of trouble. Paul says in 2 Corinthians 4:16, "Don't lose *heart*. Though outwardly we are going through it, inwardly we can constantly be made new!" (my paraphrase). Many times when we are struggling with painful situations in our lives or painful truths about ourselves, we tend to look either inside or around ourselves, and compare ourselves with other people. But be assured that looking inside or around ourselves will never change our situation. It will only cause us anxiety, magnify our weaknesses, and show us how corrupt and misaligned the thoughts that lurk inside our hearts really are.

In Psalm 73 it seems the great psalmist Asaph is going through a terrible bout of spiritual depression. He looked around and saw the wicked prospering. He even said, "They don't have troubles like the rest of us! They are braggers and they even mock God." (See verses 6–9.) This worship leader's famous song was "He Is Good." But looking around almost made his feet slip. He almost said that God was not good! In verses 21–22 Asaph said, "When *my heart* was sad and I was angry, I was senseless and stupid. I acted like an animal toward you" (ncv, emphasis added). It took a trip to the temple, where he beheld the beauty of the Lord, for Asaph to realize that God was close to him.

Asaph was slipping into a spiritual depression. The enemy almost took him out and tried to take away his song. But somehow he fixed his eyes on the Lord and continued to lead the people in anointed worship, which is what he was created to do!

Genesis 6:5 says the Lord saw that *every thought of the human heart* was inclined to evil. Note: the Lord sees every thought of the heart, and He sees its inclination. This clearly tells us why we must have Jesus come inside our hearts by the power of the Holy Spirit. It's because without Him dwelling on the inside, we don't stand a chance against the onslaught of evil that comes to wrap itself around the brains of our hearts. When we think of evil, we often think of murder, adultery, greed, selfish ambition, and lust. But there's another kind of evil in the brain of the human heart that is absolutely just as destructive. It's the evil that murders the promises of God and the hope we have in Him.

Negative thinking and imperfect, warped thoughts about a perfect, kind, and merciful God who really wants to rescue us from ourselves are probably more deadly than the kinds of evils we typically think of, yet we live with negative, warped thoughts each and every day. But it's time for a brain wash. It's time for the brains in our hearts to be thoroughly washed, daily and continually, from negative thoughts about our gracious and loving Savior.

Let's look at the life of Elijah, the most powerful prophet ever to have lived. Talk about a battle with spiritual depression. James 5:17 says, "Elijah was a human being just like us" (ncv). He was a man full of God's power but also full of weaknesses. He experienced great highs and great lows, just as we do. He came on the scene from out of nowhere. The Word tells us in 1 Kings 17 that Elijah was a man of power; at his word the rain stopped and there was a drought in Israel. This prophet's ministry was on a roll. If there were a conference circuit in those days, Elijah would definitely have top billing. He would have been considered the most influential, God-fearing man of His day. His picture would have been plastered on the cover of every spiritual magazine. He could have written a book called *How to Survive a Three-and-a-Half Year Drought and Stay Healthy at the Same Time*, and it would have been a *New York Times* best seller!

Elijah stood up to a wicked king. The Bible says King Ahab was the most wicked of all the kings of Israel. Believe me, there was a vast amount of wickedness to choose from, but Ahab came out on top. Elijah obviously was a man of courage and tenacity to have stood up to Ahab. He couldn't be swayed. He didn't have a compromising bone in His body, even if it meant his life would be in jeopardy. Yet the Bible says Elijah was a man "just like us"!

I have to admit, the previous description of Elijah doesn't quite sound like me!

Elijah said it would not rain, and just as he said, it didn't rain for three and a half years. Because Ahab was trying to kill him, Elijah hid for a season and during that time drank from a brook and received food from the mouth of a predatory raven. Then when the brook dried up, as brooks oftentimes do, Elijah received new marching orders from heaven. The Lord often allows brooks to dry up in our lives so we will not become dependent on the brook but on the One who allows the brook to give us sustenance. Didn't Jesus say, "Man shall not live by bread alone but on every word that proceeds out of the mouth of God"? (See Matthew 4:4.) That's exactly how Elijah lived—by the command of God—and without doubt or complaint he went where God directed him to go.

At this juncture of Elijah's life the Lord directed him to go to a little town called Zarephath. Let me just say a little something about this particular town. This was where King Ahab's father-in-law lived. It was the hometown of Queen Jezebel. Seriously, if you are on the run, in hiding from these very people, the last place you go and live is the small town of your archenemy's close relative. But God prepares a table for us, even in the presence of our enemies. God knows how to hide us in public.

In Zarephath Elijah's needs were met by a poor widow who had one son. When Elijah met her, she was about to make herself and her son one last meal with the little bit of flour and oil she had left, then they expected to face the same fate that was awaiting all the others around them. But this man of God came to town and asked the "poor widow" for a drink of water, and while she was getting it, he asked her for a loaf of bread.

That seems so rude and self-serving! He doesn't ask her to please give him a tiny sip of water to wet his parched lips and share with him a few crumbs of bread No, he asks for a drink—during a drought, no less—which she graciously and quickly gives him. (Can you imagine parting with your last few ounces of water in the midst of a severe drought?) Then he basically says to her, "Widow lady, while you are fetching me the water, could you get yourself home with the little bit of strength that you have and bake *me* a loaf of bread *first?* Bring it to me as I rest for a while, and then you can go back home and bake a loaf for yourself and your son" (1 Kings 17:13, my paraphrase).

He has already asked her for water, and not only does he now ask her for another precious commodity—bread—but also his request again seems extremely insensitive. He was basically saying that even though she and her son were starving, he wanted them to put their physical and emotional needs aside; go through the tedious process of baking the bread, smelling its aroma; and then leave home and return to where he was without taking a bite so he could be fed *first! Whew!* I don't know how long it took to bake a loaf of bread in those days—to knead the flour without a fancy food processor and then gather sticks to make the fire—but I'm sure it was time consuming. It's time consuming even in this day and age to bake anything, even a boxed cake!

But the widow does exactly as the prophet asked (1 Kings 17:15). *Wow!* This woman is absolutely the real hero of this story. We might take food out of our own mouths, but tell me what other mother would take food out of her child's mouth to feed a stranger who claims to be a man of God. I might be inclined to share a small piece of my loaf—a very small piece of my little loaf—but I can't imagine baking bread for someone else, taking in the aroma as it was baking over that hot fire, hearing my stomach growl, and looking into the eyes of my starving son who must have been screaming, "Mommy, what are you doing?"

Really? Ignore all these real, tangible circumstances, and give the bread to the stranger first? Realize this: Elijah wasn't gaunt or emaciated in his appearance. He had been taken care of by the Lord up to that point. The widow didn't know him. She hadn't seen his spiritual résumé. He hadn't given her any credentials from the school of the prophets! She didn't know if he was a fraud or a true man of God. After all, she could have thought to herself, "If you are a man of God, tell God to rain down manna for you."

To her Elijah was a complete stranger. But somehow this poor widow with a pure heart was rich in faith. She just took him at his word. As a matter of fact, she said, "As the Lord your God lives, I do not have bread" (1 Kings 17:12, mev). Did you notice that she said "the Lord *your* God," as though the Lord wasn't her God? At least not yet, anyway.

But I bet deep down in the recesses of her heart, because her heart was clean, because the brain inside of her heart didn't think ill thoughts, she bore witness to this man's words. I bet she somehow connected to his anointing and was prompted in her heart to trust him. It's one thing to trust God in the good times, but when the clock is ticking and your back is against the wall, that's quite a different story. I believe that as much as God wanted to save Elijah's life because he was God's man, God, knowing the pure heart of this woman, also wanted to save this woman and her son.

Before the widow agreed to make bread for Elijah, the prophet gave her a promise: "The barrel of meal will not run out, nor will the jar of oil empty, until the day that the Lord sends rain upon the earth" (v. 14, mev). *Wow!* This is just another reason to have a brain wash! Without clean hearts we miss out on so many of God's blessings because the brains in our hearts reason why we should or shouldn't obey God. Sometimes the commands of God seem so insensitive to us, but they are really just the test before the testimony! Many times the span of the test is just eighteen inches long. Often it's just a matter of winning the battle between the head and the heart.

So far as far as Elijah is concerned, things are working out according to plan. Then in 1 Kings 18 there's the showdown at Mount Carmel: Elijah against 450 prophets of Baal (as well as 400 prophets of Asherah). Elijah is fearless in the face of this challenge. He knows that he plus God is a majority, and he's confident God will send fire down from heaven and put the false god Baal to shame. Sure enough, God sends down fire from heaven, and Elijah's sacrifice is consumed even though it is the only one drenched in water. (See 1 Kings 18:16–46.)

God's people repent and shout, "The Lord, He is God! The Lord, He is God!" (v. 39, mev). Even Ahab is impressed. Finally God sends the rain, and Elijah beats Ahab to Jezreel by outrunning Ahab's chariot. Elijah is hyped up, ecstatic. Finally the nation of Israel will turn back to the Lord. This is supposed to be the happy ending, the testimony on Sunday morning! These are the things we make movies out of. This is what will promote the prophet's ministry and cause it to go global!

But Ahab went home to his wife, Jezebel (v. 46), and the queen wasn't feeling what the king was feeling. No matter how he tried to explain the move of God in the service the night before, no matter how he tried to express the magnitude of God's power, she was not moved one iota (1 Kings 19:1). And Jezebel was not one to take defeat lying down. She didn't care about fire and rain and Elijah the Olympic-caliber runner. She cared about what was done to the reputation of the king, the queen, and Baal— and so pride trumped repentance.

She brazenly threatened Elijah's life, and Elijah went on the run (v. 2). Wait a minute. *What?* No way! Elijah the great prophet, running away from Jezebel? This just cannot be! But, sad to say, there would be no testimony on Sunday morning, and the nation would remain under the thumb of a despot. Elijah, the man just like us, reached his breaking point. The man just like us hit a brick wall. Aren't men of God, especially prophets and pastors, able to leap tall buildings in a single bound? Nope. The man just like us is disappointed, discouraged, depressed, and despondent. Elijah went from faith to fear in a New York minute. The man just like us gave up the fight, and his fire went up in smoke.

If there had been church services the next day, Elijah would have been absent! He left his servant behind and then walked a day's journey into the desert, alone and isolated. Don't ever send yourself into the desert—you may never come out. It's a different story if God sends you into the desert, because where He leads you His grace will keep you. Now in the desert we see Elijah praying a different type of prayer. It's no longer the fiery prayer of faith. No, it's the pitiful prayer of fear. He cries out to God, "It is enough! Now, O Lord, take my life, for I am not better than my fathers" (v. 4, mev). This is one exhausted, battle-weary man of God. He actually said, "Take my life, Lord!" *Wow!* Mission accomplished, Jezebel!

Heartsick

What could possibly have happened? I've heard many different sermons on this subject. Some have said that it was "Monday morning blues." After such a great victory Elijah's emotions probably plummeted, and he ended up hitting rock bottom. But that doesn't seem to fit his MO, his modus operandi.

This is what I believe happened: After all was said and done, *nothing* really changed. After the brook and the ravens nourished him, after the widow's flour and oil multiplied, after the showdown at Mount Carmel, after seeing 450 prophets of Baal slaughtered, after outrunning a chariot in the midst of torrential rain—(Wow! Such victory!)—*after all was said and done*, after three and a half years of sacrifice, dedication, and getting his hopes up that even King Ahab's heart was starting to turn, Ahab and Jezebel were *still* Ahab and Jezebel!

I believe Elijah was spiritually depressed. His heart took a nosedive into the depths of despair. Disappointment precedes depression. It's amazing that God can feed us by a raven and multiply flour and oil, but He won't change someone's heart who refuses to yield to the writing on the wall.

The Bible says in Proverbs 13:12, "Hope deferred makes the heart sick." How many of us have been heartsick? How many of us have been spiritually depressed and didn't want to admit that we were going through the dark night of the soul? How many of us have been hoping for a miracle? Hoping for the spouse or the child to get saved. Hoping for the health report to turn around and for the cancer to disappear. Hoping for the child to wake up out of the coma. Hoping to conceive a baby. Hoping for the promotion— hoping, hoping, hoping!

And how many times have we been on the precipice of something amazing happening to us, and the rug of success seems to be pulled right from under us? Just when the smell of victory is right under our very noses, just when we are about to put a stake in the ground to fly the flag of victory, the enemy comes along and snatches it all away in a crushing defeat—and mocks us to boot. All our sweat, tears, dedication, and sacrifice go right down the drain. Our hopes are dashed to the ground. In the last stretch there's just no change! That is a very hard pill to swallow, especially when we are believing God for a breakthrough.

So Elijah, the man just like us, retreated from the desert to the cave of self-pity. The fact that he left his servant behind and walked inside alone was very symbolic. Leaving his servant behind seems to indicate that he was quitting the ministry. He was turning in his prophet's mantle. He took his name off the letterhead and his plaque off the office door. No more need for an assistant, no more need to have someone go before him to announce his intentions— there wouldn't be anything to assist.

In the cave he cried out from the depths of his soul, "I have been very zealous for the Lord, Lord of Hosts, for the children of Israel have forsaken Your covenant, thrown down Your altars, and killed Your prophets with the sword; and I alone am left, and they seek to take my life" (1 Kings 19:10, mev). In other words, "I've been the only one, Lord, who has stood faithful and fervent. I'm the only one going through this. Nobody knows the trouble I've seen."

Why is this happening to me? Satan loves when we go into the cave of self-pity. He loves when we isolate ourselves and never ask others to help us pray. As a matter of fact, he'll even show us the way inside the cave. Thank God the angel showed up and spoke to Elijah's heart and straightened him out! The angel says, "What are you doing here? And by the way, Elijah, you are not the only one. There are seven thousand prophets in Israel who have not bowed their knees to Baal." (See 1 Kings 19:13, 18.)

Think of the catastrophe that would have taken place if Elijah hadn't listened to the angel. How many times has the Lord sent us His word through an angel dressed in the form of a preacher or teacher, or just a coworker or someone riding on the bus with us, and because we are in such pain and despair, we shut off the spiritual ears of our hearts? Faith comes by hearing the Word of God (*in our hearts*; Psalm 119:11 says we hide His Word in our hearts so we won't sin against Him). Our hearts must be refreshed by the Word of God daily so the toxins of yesterday find no root in our hearts today.

There's always a way out of the valley, out of the desert, out of the cave! Jesus said, "In this world you will have trouble. *But take heart!* I have overcome the world" (John 16:33, emphasis added). Jesus could have said, "Don't lose your mind," but He didn't. He said, "Don't lose heart." Don't allow overwhelming thoughts that cause anxiety to settle in your heart and cause you to spiral down into spiritual depression.

I've been in that cave many a time, as I'm sure you may have been or maybe still are. Like you, I've been disappointed and wanted to roll up in a ball of despair, shut off the lights, and sleep until my time on earth was at its end. I've thought things would have gone a different way and allowed myself to lose heart because of it, only to find out in the end that God's way really is perfect. My disappointments have not only been God's appointments; those heavy weights have also given me the muscle of faith that I needed for my future. Although we encounter many valleys, crevices, and steep roads, God always brings us out. He always leads us into triumphant procession, as 2 Corinthians 2:14 declares.

My first grandson was born on the Asperger's spectrum. We were devastated. But our family, by God's grace, turned lemons into lemonade. We now have implemented a Champions Club, which originated in Lakewood Church, as a ministry in our church. During each of the services people in our congregation are trained to teach children with special needs. We now welcome dozens and dozens of families who couldn't go to church because there was no place for their children. Had our family not gone through such a time of heartache, we never would have been aware of this whole community. Our pain has become someone else's gain.

Our grandson is one of the most spectacular people you will ever meet. He is not only a genius, but he also defies the "autistic" label that has been placed on him. He is not only warm, but he is also the kindest kid alive. In the next chapter I will speak about my heartache regarding my three sons who were raised up in the house of the Lord, and how the Lord ultimately used that pain to further His kingdom!

You and I have no other choice except to heed the command the angel gave Elijah. In 1 Kings 19 the angel first touched Elijah gently and told him to eat. When Elijah looked up he saw that the angel had brought a cake of bread and a jar of water. (Even angels know that the way to a man's heart is through his stomach!) But Elijah was in such despair, he lay back down. Maybe the food needed a little garlic and a touch of olive oil!

A second time the angel came and touched Elijah, and again told him to arise and eat, for the journey would be long and he would need to get his strength. The angel was preparing him for the road ahead. He was telling him that he wasn't going to be allowed to stay in the cave and retire. This wasn't quitting time! This time Elijah ate, and he was sustained for a forty-day journey to Mount Horeb, the mountain of God. And that is where God spoke to him in a still, small voice (vv. 11–13). When we are going through a spiritual depression, we have to get to God and hear His still, small voice. That still, small voice speaks volumes and echoes throughout the core of our very being, chasing away the darkness inside.

Elijah was instructed to go back the way he came. And he was told that when he got where he was being sent, he was to anoint others (vv. 14–15). Think about how we could glean from these instructions when we are in a spiritual depression: "Go back the way you came." In other words, change direction, make an about-face, and go forward in the right direction. Get back to your post.

The Lord also told Elijah to anoint others. In other words, He was saying, "You are a prophet, and a prophet's job is to anoint others, so get back to work!" *Wow!* God knows there is so much power when we empower others. When you get the brain in your heart thinking about doing good to others and anointing other people instead of continually thinking about your own problems, that's when there's "life" in your life. The angel was basically telling Elijah that although he felt like it was the end and he wanted to give up, God wasn't done using his life. There was a lot more life inside of Elijah, and the Lord was going to make sure he didn't leave this earth until every ounce of anointing that was inside him was poured out on others.

We weren't created for defeat. That's why we don't feel good when we are living in it! We were made for more than that. We were created to be life-givers, because the giver of life lives within us. God's Word says, "Wherever there is a carcass, there the vultures will gather" (Matt. 24:28). When vultures see the frame of what was once a healthy man, they circle around and around us, waiting to swoop down and devour what's left. Satan smells depression, and he is drawn to defeat, just as God smells faith and is drawn to it.

The enemy looks for a lack of movement, and he circles around waiting for the right time to swoop down and finish us off. But the Lord looks for someone whose *heart* is fully committed to Him. That's why we cannot stay spiritually depressed. We must get up! You and I weren't intended to be food for the enemy. We were created to be bread for the spiritually famished. As long as we remain in the cave of self-pity, the spirit of Jezebel is allowed to reign, and thus sin is allowed to prevail. Ultimately the enemy will have the last laugh over our lives, and worst of all, we will make peace with our situation and stop fighting the good fight of faith!

One of the men Elijah anointed was a man named Jehu. He was a wild man—fearless—and he went after Jezebel with all of his might, but he didn't go alone. He went with a company of men. In layman's terms, he took a posse. Jehu and his band of men rode through many towns looking for her. Every time he got to a certain place, the people would ask him, "Do you come in peace?" Jehu's answer was always the same: "What does peace have to do with harlotry and whoredom?" (See 2 Kings 9:22.)

Jehu didn't stop until Jezebel was thrown down from her high place by the very ones she castrated. Can we see the wisdom Jehu used in not going it alone? Do you think Jehu saw the chink in Elijah's armor, the weak link in his ministry? Do you think that's why he gathered a group who had the same purpose, men who were like-minded and as focused as he was? I think one vital lesson we can certainly learn here is not to go it alone. No matter how much power we have by ourselves, there is strength in numbers. That's why God has given us a whole body of believers, people who are likeminded, focused, and ready to hold one another's hands up in prayer.

Elijah, the man "just like us," had the same weaknesses, faced the same enemies as we do, and got as discouraged as we may get. But we must not forget that no matter how tough things get, we have the same resources and the same power that Elijah had. We have the Holy Spirit and the body of Christ to help us fight our battles!

The one mistake Elijah made was thinking he was the only one going through a hard time. He needed the brain of his heart to be thoroughly cleansed. He definitely needed a brain wash. He was eighteen inches from victory.

Don't we often make the same mistake Elijah made? We fight our battles in secret. We fight and fight until we are worn out, then burned out and spiritually depressed. Perhaps we fight our battles alone because we think we are the only ones facing certain challenges, so we isolate ourselves, withdrawing in shame and defeat, making peace with our glum situations, and settling for less than God's best. Have you ever withdrawn from the body of Christ and stopped going to church because you felt ashamed that things didn't work out as planned? Shouldn't we be doing the exact opposite?

Just as Elijah should have called on those seven thousand prophets to defeat Jezebel, so should we call on our church family and get them to fight with us in prayer. Open your eyes. You are not alone, nor are you the only one going through hard times. We would be far better off if we tapped into the resources that are right at our fingertips. We should lock arms and form prayer groups until that spirit of Jezebel is thrown down from her high place. It's wartime, not peacetime!

Let's Pray

Lord, heal me from this spiritual depression that has taken root inside my heart. Teach me how to train my inner man to look upward instead of looking inward. Teach me to fix my eyes on You. Give me the courage not to make peace with my situation. When my heart is overwhelmed with the troubles of life, lead me to the Rock, Christ Jesus. Don't allow me to settle for anything less than Your best for my life. I'm asking that You give me the strategy to take down every high place that mocks Your name so I can have Your peace that guards my heart and my mind. And finally, Lord, give me a cheerful heart, which is good medicine—for any lingering spiritual depression. In Jesus's name, amen.

Maria Durso

CHAPTER 12 – STAND UP!

Whithen we watch Christian TV or hear sermons, much of what we see and hear in those thirty-minute segments are bona fide miracles wrought by the hand of God. Of course these testimonies are very exciting and inspiring, and they cause our hearts to soar. But what time doesn't permit to be shared are all the gory details that led up to the point of victory. Yes, there is a lot of *gory* before the *glory*! It's just like in the Old Testament; bloody battles had to be fought before the Israelites could walk off with the spoils. Things got very messy. It's great to read a scripture that says Moses stretched out his hand over the waters and the Red Sea parted (Exod. 14:21). But oh, the tension, the fear, the chaos that must have ensued as a million-plus people heard the hoofs of Egypt's horses gaining ground on them.

In many of our cases, before there was ever a message spoken on a Sunday morning, there first was a royal mess—a bloody, sweaty mess that I'm sure involved chaos and fear. There were probably many long nights of weeping before the joy came in the morning! I'm sure there was a long time span when the battle of faith was being fought in the secret place. And I'm sure that testimony cost the "testimony giver" much blood, sweat, and tears as he partnered with God, holding on to his faith as he whiteknuckled it all the way to victory. If we don't recognize this vital truth, we will wonder why our problems aren't solved in time for the next week's Sunday service. We then will compare ourselves to the "victors," the "victorious ones." We perceive these individuals to have received their instant answer to their very complex and near-impossible situation, thus causing us to live in defeat and ultimately be named amongst the quitters. Hebrews 12:3 says, "Consider him who endured such opposition from sinners, so that you will not grow weary and *lose heart*" (emphasis added).

Allow me to illustrate this point with the story of a God-fearing woman named Hannah. (See 1 Samuel 1–3.) Before we delve into her life, let me just say that there are so many Hannahs in the body of Christ. Truth be told, there are many wonderful, faithful, determined believers who serve the Lord through the good, the bad, and the ugly, regardless of the cold, hard fact that their circumstances seem either to have them in a holding pattern or to worsen before they see the light at the end of their tunnel. Yet these very ones serve the Lord just because He's their God. They live with the hope that one day will be "their day" to declare what the Lord has done for them. They live by faith, holding on to the promises of God, knowing that the Lord has an "appointed time" when the clocks of heaven and earth come into perfect synchronization.

Unfortunately, too many people do not realize that there is such a thing as an appointed time because we live in the day of instant gratification. Our culture has set us up for the immediate. We are no longer wired for "the wait." We are wired for "the instant." We tap our foot at the microwave. Years ago if you were away from home and wanted to make a phone call, you had to go to a phone booth. And you had to have the right coins to place in the change slots. If you didn't have the right change, you'd have to walk a number of city blocks to a store (very few New Yorkers had cars). When you finally got to the store, you were then subject to the store clerk's mood. The big question was, would the clerk feel like being gracious to you that day? And then, would you feel obliged to buy an item in order to be given the change requested?

If you did indeed find the change, you then had to find your way back to the phone booth. Chances were that someone prepared, unlike yourself, was now in the phone booth and had plenty of nickels to place in the slot every three minutes to keep the operator from saying in that nasally tone, "Please deposit five cents for the next three minutes!" This would allow the prepared caller's conversation to keep on going and going and going. While you're waiting, the caller would probably conveniently place his back to you so he wouldn't have to see you waiting for the phone in either the freezing cold or the sweltering heat.

When it was finally your turn to make your call, chances were that you were in such a hurry you missed the coin slot and had to bend down in those tight quarters to find the coin you dropped. *Whew!* I don't know how it was in other parts of the country, but the floor inside New York phone booths would now be considered contaminated—sticky gum, spilled drinks, rotten food pushed in the corners, and sometimes urine. I'm surprised no one lobbied Washington insisting that we be decontaminated every time we exited one of those incubuses of germs, bacteria, and viruses!

When you finally got the coin in the slot and dialed the number on the clumsy circular dial, you were probably holding your breath hoping you didn't get the dreaded busy signal on the other end! Yes, there was such a thing as a busy signal, that annoying tone that modulated up and down, clearly indicating that this is a no-go; try again later! *Help!*

Of course you didn't always get a busy signal, but many times the wait seemed endless until someone finally picked up on the other end. The creators of the cell phone made sure their customers didn't have this traumatic experience. We simply don't have busy signals. We now just leave a voicemail, send a text, or shoot an e-mail, and the response is usually— yes, you guessed it—"instant!"

So what are we to do? People in this day and age aren't wired to wait. Yet without "the wait" our strength won't be renewed. As the Bible declares in Isaiah 40:31, those who wait upon the Lord will not only renew their strength, but they will also mount up with wings like an eagle, they will run and not be weary, and they will walk but not faint! The Bible also tells us that the trials we go through in life are not in vain. Those are the very things that work in us patience so we will be lacking nothing (James 1:4). Let me be clear: the Lord doesn't cause the wait to develop our character; the character that is developed in us during the wait is the icing on the cake as we wait for God's appointed time!

Now, I don't know about you, but if you are anything like me, you probably don't like to hear the word *wait*, especially when it's in the same sentence as *trials* and *patience*. The word *wait* is absolutely the worst four-letter word, especially when we don't tack on the only two words that make waiting palatable: "a moment." Wait a moment, and I will be right with you! *Ah*, that's the only way I like to hear that four-letter word used. I don't like "wait until." What do you mean "until"? Until what? Until when?

Habakkuk 2:3 says, "For the vision is yet for an *appointed time*; but it speaks of the end, and does not lie. *If it delays, wait for it*; it will *surely come, it will not delay*" (mev, emphasis added). I do not like what this scripture is implying! What do you mean by "though it linger"? The thought of it is making me twitch! The word *linger*, which is sometimes translated "tarry," seems to contradict the words "will not delay." If I have to tarry or wait for it because it is lingering, then in my mind it is already delayed!

But all kidding aside, you and I know that God knows the exact time your miracle is to come, because that miracle isn't just for you; it's for the people around you in your sphere of influence. There is, without a doubt, a "divinely appointed time" on heaven's calendar for your faith to become sight, when the people who have witnessed firsthand the gory circumstances in your life will be able to see up close and personal the glory of what could only be an intervention by the hand of God.

Barren and Broken

In 1 Samuel 1 we read about a woman who knew a lot about waiting. The Bible says Elkanah had two wives (uh-oh!). The first was Hannah and the second was Peninnah. Peninnah had children, but Hannah had none. Peninnah taunted Hannah cruelly, rubbing it in and never letting her forget that God had not given her children. This went on *year after year*! (See 1 Samuel 1:1–2, 6–7.)

Looking at Scripture, it is plain to see that there are some things in life— yes, even in the life of a godly believer—that are chronic. There are issues in life that are beyond our control. It is what it is for the time being. The Bible says that Hannah's unfortunate circumstance went on *year after year*. That implies that there was just no relief for this God-fearing woman. But

God had an appointed time. Did Hannah know that? Did she know she was going to give birth to a prophet who would change Israel? Of course not. Like most of us, she probably couldn't see beyond her pain and grief, but she held on to God for dear life.

If we fail to understand that bad or sad, unfair or unjust things happen to good people, we will be crippled. We will think that there is something wrong with us. We will think deep down in our hearts that God is against us. Distorted thinking such as this will end up paralyzing and discouraging us. Think about Abraham and Sarah. What a chronic situation—twenty-five years of chronic. And you can't think about years and years of injustice and not think about Joseph, the God-fearing young man who went from the pit to the prison before he ever got to the palace.

We sometimes think that if God truly loves us, then we'll never have a problem in the world. Or we think if we're living right, then God will cause everything in our lives to be perfect. This is simply not true! Don't drink the Kool-Aid! Jesus Himself said that in this world, we will absolutely, definitely, without a doubt have troubles. But He also said, *"Don't lose heart; I have overcome the world."* (See John 16:33.)

Hannah was a woman who loved God, and God loved her, yet she was not exempt from heartache and a long season of discouraging drought. Even though she had severe domestic troubles, she was still faithful to serve the Lord. She never took a position that said, "Well, God hasn't answered my prayer, so why should I serve Him? Or, "God hasn't relieved me of my enemy, so why should I go up to the house of the Lord and worship Him?" No, Hannah wasn't a quitter. She was steadfast, immovable, always abounding in the work of the Lord. She didn't serve God for what He could give her; she served God because of who He was!

Unfortunately today people have to be baited to believe in Jesus. We tell them that if you come to the Lord, He will give you thus and so, instead of telling them what He has already given them and letting them know that if He never did another thing for them, He'd already have done more than any of us would ever deserve. He's already done more than enough!

The Bible tells us that Hannah was barren. In those days that was the equivalent of being a leper. As a matter of fact, you were better off being a leper. Lepers lived outside of town in a leper colony with others who were infected. Hannah had the privilege of living right in town so everyone in her community could glare at her. After all, you couldn't rent children to avoid walking to the market alone.

I'm sure that along with the stares, there were whispers. There was a stigma attached to being barren. Barrenness meant that you were different, peculiar. It was a source of disgrace. A barren wife was seen as an embarrassment—damaged goods, defective. Beyond the shame and humiliation, barrenness caused people to wonder: Is it because of God's judgment? Is there sin in her life? Does God want to end that lineage? Imagine the guilt Hannah must have felt. And to add insult to injury, the Bible says in 1 Samuel 1:6 that the Lord had closed up her womb. In other words, Hannah's barrenness was God's doing! God was allowing this horrific predicament!

Because Hannah was barren, her husband, Elkanah, took another wife to carry on the family name. Elkanah was a Levite from a priestly line called the Kohathites. Under the Jewish law he was permitted to take on another wife to produce offspring to continue the priestly line. Hannah must have felt like a failure on multiple fronts. She must have thought that she was a disappointment not only physically but also spiritually, because she deprived her husband of being able to carry on his godly seed.

So now Peninnah becomes part of this equation, adding another layer of pain to Hannah's brokenness. Doesn't it seem that unfortunate circumstances oftentimes lead to more unfortunate circumstances? When it rains, it pours! The Bible says that Peninnah had children. First Samuel 1:4 refers to "all her sons and daughters," implying that her quiver was full. Peninnah is a regular baby-making machine. She is spitting those babies out one after the other.

Bible commentators believe Peninnah had at least four sons and two daughters. We know that in biblical times having numerous children was a symbol of status and wealth. So let's do the math. If Peninnah had at least six children, with nine months of pregnancy for each, and time for her body to rest and a period for weaning the baby between each birth, she must have been taunting Hannah for ten to twelve years.

To the natural eye Peninnah was blessed and loved by God, and Hannah was not. Isn't that the rational conclusion many people would draw? Don't people often judge whether a person is blessed by the car they drive, the zip code they live in, the amount on their bank statement, or the size of the diamond on their finger? This is just another indication that the brains in our hearts needs to be scrubbed clean! We should never, ever judge who is blessed and who is not, or who is loved by God and who is not, by outward circumstances. As we discussed in chapter 5, Jesus's mother, Mary, had her baby in a stable, and the Bible says she was blessed among women! Let's call blessed what God calls blessed!

In 1 Samuel 1:7 the Bible says that *every time* Elkanah took his family up to the sanctuary of God, Hannah expected to be taunted by Peninnah. She'd rub it in, never letting Hannah forget that God had not given her children. How cruel. *Every time.* Not some of the time or most of the time—no, the Bible says *every time* they went to worship, Peninnah taunted and ridiculed Hannah.

Peninnah made sure that by the time Hannah got up to the tabernacle to worship the Lord, she was so heartsick that her short time in God's presence would be ruined. Good ole Peninnah capitalized on Hannah's pain, flaunted her blessings, and made sure Hannah knew God was the cause of it all! Talk about a pleasant church experience. Every time she went to worship the Lord, she was tormented, agitated, humiliated, and jeered. Every time she went to hear from heaven, there was just no time for rest. How could she even *want* to hear from a God who had the power to end her humiliation yet stood by in deafening silence, seeming to do nothing?

The Bible says Peninnah provoked Hannah sore, until she would not eat (1 Sam. 1:7). By the time Hannah got in the presence of the Lord, she was completely distraught. Let's process what this is implying. The whole family was going up to the tabernacle of God, where the ark of the covenant, the mercy seat, and the amazing, glorious presence of the Lord were. "They"—all of them together as one big, unhappy family—were going to worship the Lord! That was the goal: to sing praises to the Lord! Imagine that. Peninnah was a churchgoer, a tabernacle member, a believer in Jehovah God. This tells me that just because people go to worship, that doesn't mean they are worshippers. It tells me that God's house is inhabited by the sincere and the insincere. In God's house there are many Hannahs, but unfortunately there are a few too many Peninnahs too.

Peninnah was what we would call a "church bully." They do exist, you know! Some people actually come to church to show off their gifts and talents and to draw attention to themselves. Some people come to church to flaunt their blessings and let you know that they are God's number one. For some people this kind of behavior is premeditated; they come to church to cause grief. Some people come to the house of the Lord to be vindictive and cruel, or to exert their authority. For some people performing the "act of worship," it's just an act. Sometimes your greatest stumbling block is sitting in the pew right next to you in the house of the Lord. Sometimes wounded people are wounded over and over again because attending church just reminds them that God hasn't answered their prayer. One preacher said a long time ago, "Many are the tears shed in the sanctuary."

But let's take a quick second to examine the underpinnings of someone like Peninnah. What sort of person does things like that? The Bible says in Luke 6:43–45, "A good tree does not corrupt fruit, nor does a corrupt tree bear good fruit. Each tree is known by its own fruit. Men do not gather figs from thorns, nor do they gather grapes from a wild bush. A good man *out of the good treasure of his heart* bears what is good, and an evil man *out of the evil treasure of his heart* bears what is evil. For of the *abundance of the heart* his mouth speaks" (mev, emphasis added).

Wow! Dirty heart, dirty mouth. Evil heart, evil actions. Our hearts must be attached to the good tree, which is Christ Jesus. Disconnected from Him, we will be people like Peninnah, people who *go* to church instead of people who *are* the church. How many people are members of Christ-centered, Bible-believing churches but are racists? How many are real troublemakers? How many are gossipers and slanderers? How many are parts of cliques within their churches, wanting to be the "popular ones" and treating church as though it were the high school lunchroom? How many suffer from the disease of jealousy, hoping someone falls flat on his face so they can sing the solo? How many have their pastor for Sunday dinner? (And I don't mean *over* for Sunday dinner; unfortunately they eat him alive with their hurtful criticism.) How many make fun of the less fortunate, sneering at them and turning their prideful noses up at those who are not pretty, wealthy, or mentally up to par?

Peninnah was disconnected from the only tree that can cause one to bear good fruit. You and I must make sure the roots of our hearts stay attached to the tree of the Lord. We must guard our hearts continuously, pruning the roots and making sure we remain within the parameters of holy ground, inside the boundaries of the garden of God. Once we stray onto enemy territory, we will become rooted in the wrong soil. We will then produce evil, prideful, and self-righteous actions, most likely causing pain to those around us and tarnishing the name of Christ.

Hannah had it rough. Her pain wasn't confined to Ramah, which was her hometown. No, everywhere Hannah went, her pain was sure to go. Her pain followed her all the way to Shiloh, where the tabernacle was. Shiloh should bring relief, but instead she was ridiculed and reduced to tears and unable to eat. These were not the tears and fasting of a woman of faith. No, these were tears of humiliation.

Can you imagine being so discouraged that you can get to God's house but never get to God? The waters of refreshing are all around you, but you still leave dry. The meat of God's Word is before you, but you're too weak to digest what is being said. And here's the ironic part: year after year she was a stone's throw away from the presence of God—the inner court, where the ark was kept—yet she never made contact with the living God. Year after year she went up, but she never went in! Year after year she left the same way she came. Year after year she went back home without asking for what she needed from the only One who could grant her petition.

But 1 Samuel 1:9 says that one day Hannah stood up. One day, after all those years, Hannah took a stand. One day Hannah said, "Enough is enough!" One day faith replaced discouragement. One day Hannah changed her posture! When someone stands, they're saying, "It's over! Enough is enough! I'm not taking this sitting down any longer. I'm taking authority."

Our girl Hannah got some sanctified aggression. She decided, "I don't have to sit at the table of grief and despair when I could be sitting in the presence of the Lord." Satan loves when we are sitting when we should be standing up, getting to God, and praying. One day the light went on for Hannah. She must have thought that if God opened the wombs of Sarah and Rachel, then He could do it for her! She wasn't going to stand for the status quo any longer!

So she ran into the tabernacle—no more outer court for Hannah. No more traditions of man. No more "dead orthodoxy"! Hannah defied the protocol of the day. Though she was a "mere" woman, she experienced a divine transaction. She made contact with heaven! And she experienced a holy explosion. She stopped crying over what she didn't have and started to cry out for what she could have. Out of her anguish and grief she released a cry that got heaven's attention.

Now Eli the priest thought she was drunk. *He was sitting.* The priest of the tabernacle was sitting down on the job. And because he was sitting instead of standing in God's presence, he lost his discernment, his spiritual compass. Imagine this. This woman finally gets the chutzpah to go into God's presence. She finally has the faith to cry out to Him, and here comes the "priest," the "leader," the "pastor," casting judgment on her actions.

As leaders we cannot be reclining and fall asleep in the light. If we do, we will misunderstand people and limit God's power. The priest's actions could have totally derailed Hannah. But Hannah kept standing! Her faith would not be deterred! This time she stood in humility before Eli the priest and she said, "Let your handmaid find grace in your sight" (1 Sam. 1:18, mev). Leaders, the people following you, the people in your ministry, are looking for affirmation from you, not criticism. May we have anointed eyes to see both the people's pain and their potential.

The Bible says in verse 18 that when Hannah left the tabernacle, her face was no longer downcast. Hannah was no longer eighteen inches from victory. This is the trademark of faith. When Hannah left, she knew the Lord was going to give her exactly what she asked for. She went home and ate a victory meal even before she actually saw the victory. We need to eat more victory meals and do a little celebrating before we see the "baby bump."

And consider this: Hannah asked for a son, and God gave her a prophet. He always gives us much more than we could ask, think, or imagine! (See Ephesians 3:20–21.) It was well worth the wait!

Hannah wasn't the only one who was due. Israel was due for a man of God to change the nation. Thus, the appointed time. The gory turned into glory!

The Gift Of Faith

I'm sure many of us can relate to Hannah. I know I can. You don't have to be childless to know barrenness. I loved the Lord and served Him from the moment I got saved. But that didn't exempt me from heartache. God in His mercy gave me three amazing sons, and I raised them up in the house of the Lord. My boys grew up on the pew of the church, so to speak. The only two churches they ever knew were the Brooklyn Tabernacle and then Christ Tabernacle. They experienced powerful prayer meetings and mighty moves of God. They were birthed in an incubator of God's presence where the people around them were hot for God.

What my husband and I lived at church, we lived at home. There was no compromise. They witnessed us praying for Saturday baseball teams to open in our neighborhood so they could join, because in our home Sunday was the Lord's Day. They saw firsthand how God opened those doors for them. They saw how when my oldest son, Adam, joined the Cub Scouts, I got the uniform and sewed the patches on, but the night I was to send him, the Holy Spirit told me to hang the uniform back up because he was not to go. I obeyed that still, small voice, only to find out later on that month that the man in charge of his troop was molesting the children.

God never failed to lead us. The boys saw the greatest sinners become the greatest saints right before their eyes! They were gang members and drug dealers one moment and choir members the next! They saw how God provided for us when we first went into the ministry because my husband's parents disowned us. They saw me cry out to God for a steak one night. I said, "Lord, if I eat another egg, I'm gonna cackle and grow feathers." They saw that evening the doorbell ring and someone hand me thick-cut, juicy steaks. The person said, "We were going to eat these, but all of a sudden we wanted to go out to eat." You talk about a victory meal! (See 1 Samuel 1:18.)

Another time we didn't have any bread in the house, and I didn't have any money to buy some to make my kids their peanut butter and jelly sandwiches for the next day's lunch. That happened to be the night of our prayer meeting. I heard the Holy Spirit say, "Just go to the meeting." I did, and lo and behold, a woman who still attends our church was standing in the vestibule of our old building with a loaf of bread in her hands. She was tall and was holding the loaf up high, saying, "Does anyone need a loaf of bread?" I said, "That's my bread!"

They also witnessed their grandpa and grandma get miraculously saved and provide the money needed to buy the office building where we now house our staff. That doesn't seem so amazing, except that for a time my in-laws cut us off when we went into the ministry. My husband, who was the oldest of three sons, worked for them. The family has an Italian gourmet food business, which was, by the way, on *Throwdown! with Bobby Flay*. (That was a shameless plug, I know.) Well, when my husband decided to go into the ministry, my in-laws took it very personally. They felt like my husband betrayed them to go work for Jim Cymbala, sort of like leaving one family for another one. They didn't see it as a decision to serve the Lord. So they cut us off so their son would come back.

The church paid us $80 per week, plus they paid our mortgage (which was $287 per month) and our utilities. We went from making $1,000 a week with paid vacations to one of their vacation properties, company cars, and yearly bonuses to making $80 a week with no insurance and no vacations. It was like the rug of security was pulled right from underneath us. But years later the gory became the glory! God, as usual, was so faithful. Slow but faithful!

When my oldest son, Adam, reached his early teenage years, something started to change. It was like *Transformers*—he changed; his countenance changed. As he got a little older, he became a bit more defiant. Because sin is infectious and cannot be contained, it affected the other two boys. Here I am serving God wholeheartedly. I'm a pastor's wife, a ministry leader, and a sought-after speaker for women's conferences, and out of nowhere trouble comes to my house. It was like a plague, a very dark time, and it turned out to be a chronic situation for quite a number of years. My house was full of physical children, but it was void of spiritual life.

My husband loved me and our church was growing, but I had another reason to feel ashamed and disgraced. I felt as though I had failed. During the Sunday services the tradition was for the pastor's family to be on the front row. During the glorious worship time I would be lost in God, only to open my eyes and see my sons missing in action. I wanted to run out and chase after them, but all eyes were on me, so I had to sit calmly in my seat as though everything was all right. Of course, week after week my time in the presence of God was ruined. I couldn't concentrate. I was plagued with guilt. What kind of mother was I? What kind of kids did I raise? How did I mess up so royally? I would tell my husband, "Maybe we should step down from the ministry."

"Intercessory prayer ministry leader? Ha! What a joke!" the enemy taunted me. Whether I was at home or at church, I couldn't escape the shame that I felt. Someone in my congregation told me that God showed him there was sin in my life and that we weren't people of faith. Nothing like a word of encouragement when you are already crawling on the ground feeling like you can't get any lower! This went on year after year. I cried buckets at the altar, but nothing changed *because I didn't change!* I left church and picked up the same ole carnal weapons week after week and year after year. My weapons of choice were nagging, complaining, self-pity, self-righteousness, guilt, and, of course, condemnation.

Let me just say that one of the many lessons I've learned is that God is not moved by our whining or self-pity. It may work with your husband, friends, or kids, but it absolutely does not work with God. The one and only thing that works with God is for His holy nostrils to smell faith! I've also learned that I'm not the only one suffering from this plague of self-pity. It has spread worldwide, and it is to date the greatest threat to seeing the next generation step up and take the lead.

Sometimes—or should I say, oftentimes—we go to church but we don't go to war! Sometimes we are so busy crying that we have forgotten how to cry out! I remember thinking that having a vibrant youth ministry would be the answer to my kids' problems. So our church's prayer ministry cried out for many years: "God, please give us a vibrant youth ministry. Give us a youth choir!" But year after year there was no sign of life. It was as though God shut up the heavens. It was as though the womb of our prayers couldn't produce life.

The enemy would provoke me. I would hear a voice deep within say, "That's not for you. That's not for your church. That'll never happen for you." I would white-knuckle it and pitifully tell the intercessors, "I know it seems as though the heavens are as brass, but I believe that one day God just might hear our cry." That was as much faith as I could muster!

But one day I stood up! One day I pushed myself away from the table of grief and accusation and shame! One day as I was reading my morning devotions, I read these words from Hebrews 3:6, "But Christ is faithful as Son over God's house. And we are his house." I stopped in my tracks as the Holy Spirit struck me deep in my heart! As I read the words, "*We are his house,*" the Holy Spirit continued the sentence and said these life-changing words: "*And My house shall be called a house of prayer, but you have made it a den of thieves!*"

I immediately got defensive. I said, "Me, Lord? *Me?*" I thought, "I'm the head of the intercessory prayer ministry; that's the Navy SEALs, the Special Forces, don't You know?" The Holy Spirit quickly answered me that day and said, "*You are praying nice mothers' prayers—prayers like, 'He's a good boy.' No, he's not. 'It's just a phase.' No, it's not! Your sons are in big trouble! You are trying put out a nuclear war with a BB gun. You need to go to war. You need to fast and pray! A life for a life!*"

I should have felt energized by those words. After all, the Lord was giving me the key to ending this bloody battle. But instead I felt resentment and couldn't understand why at first. I immediately retorted and said, "I raised my boys up in the house of the Lord, and I have done everything possible." There was silence! I pushed away from the kitchen table and walked into the dining room (you know, the one with the leak!). I then said to God, "I would pray and fast, but I really don't believe that You would save my children!"

Oh, you see, I could easily believe that God would save *your* child, but not mine. The brain in my heart wasn't wired to receive blessings. It was wired to expect the worst or to expect nothing when it came to something that mattered to me. I told God that day, "The truth is, I know you saved Franklin Graham, the great Billy Graham's son, because he's Billy Graham's son. And I know you saved Pastor Cymbala's daughter Chrissy, because she's Pastor Cymbala's daughter. But Lord, I don't believe You would save my sons because they are mine, and I am damaged."

I felt my husband and I were just a couple of ex-druggies. Way down deep inside my heart I didn't believe we were worth what these other families were worth. I mean, we were lucky that we were saved, and I didn't want to push my luck. I didn't think God could ever use my family. We didn't have a great spiritual heritage.

Then a light went on, and I had a life-changing revelation that rewired the way the brain in my heart thought. I realized that faith wasn't a fruit of the Spirit; it was a gift from God! I didn't have to wait twenty years to cultivate it. I didn't have to pray the three right things in the right order to have my prayer answered. I didn't have to earn it, and I couldn't get it by pretending that I had it. No! If, in fact, I didn't have faith—and I didn't— all I had to do was go to the Giver of the gift and ask Him for it! It was as simple as that. I just had to admit that I didn't have faith to believe for my children to turn around. I simply had to go to the only One who could change my situation and ask Him to give me the weapon of faith to tear down this chronic issue.

After that revelation I prayed the simplest and shortest prayer I'd ever prayed in my life: "Lord, baptize me with the gift of faith!" I promise you, that day in my dining room the Holy Spirit baptized me with faith from the top of my head to the soles of my feet! I felt electrified! I knew, like Hannah, that I was going to receive what I had prayed for! From that moment on everything seemed different. It was as though this cloud of darkness left. I could see clearly. I saw my sons as the mighty men of God they were destined to be. God gave me this supernatural gift of faith to believe His Word. I was now a believer, no longer a disbeliever.

I knew that I was now pregnant with new life in my spiritual womb. The spiritual pregnancy test came out *positive*, and I was positive that I'd give birth in the spirit! I went to war! My motto was *enough is enough*! Now it was time for me to nurture this growing promise that I was carrying. I changed my posture. I stopped crying over what I didn't have, and I started to cry out over what I could have. I fasted. While cooking for my family, I would hear the Holy Spirit say, "Don't eat that. A life for a life. Eat soup. Eat a salad. Eat an egg." And most of all, "*Go to war!*"

When everyone left the house, I turned into Attila the Hun! I stopped praying "nice mothers' prayers." No more Mrs. Nice Gal! I called those things in my kids' lives exactly what they were—no sugar-coating! I started to come against the spirit of pride, manipulation, lust, and plain ole worldliness! God started to reveal very specific things to me. My oldest son, Adam, was involved in dealing drugs; my middle son, Jordan, was getting involved in gang activity, painting graffiti all over the neighborhood; and my youngest son, Chris, was following in his brothers' footsteps. Adam would come home, and I would say, "Excuse me, I have to look in that pocket," and I would pull out a marijuana joint! I had no need to nag. I couldn't be deterred. I would simply say, "You have a good night now, son."

Now my kids were looking at me as though I was an alien! I kind of was. I was carrying something from another world inside of me, and it was fueling me! One night when my youngest son, Chris, was spending the night at a friend's house, I was quickened in the wee hours to call that house, which I did. As the friend answered the phone, he said to my son, "It's your mother." I told my son, "Don't you dare look at that magazine." And then I hung up the phone. Similar things happened with my son Jordan. He came home from a party one night, and I said, "Jordan, I know exactly what you did tonight." He was my most tender son. He would come home and find me on my knees and say, "Mom, please don't stop praying for me. It's working."

Suddenly my kids saw the hand of God for themselves. They started to realize that God was much more than a "church thing"! God was real, and He was blowing up their spot. But let me add the most important thing that accompanied my radical change of heart: my prayer ministry went to war with me. They joined forces and locked arms with me, and we went to war as a force to be reckoned with. We were determined to fight down this enemy and destroy this plague. We got a piece of oak tag and drew a huge bull's-eye in the center. I put my kids' names and their friends' names right in the center, and others added their children's names! We even added the names of some whose parents were not represented. Some parents were so resentful that their little darlings' names were included amongst the lost, they demanded that we take the names down. We obliged. I said, "Suit yourself." But I added these words: "I don't care if I have to take out a centerfold ad in the *Daily News*; my kids *will serve the Lord*."

Now all our prayers changed. We were all on fire, set ablaze. We were on a mission, and we knew that the mission would be accomplished. It so happens that things seemed to get worse with my oldest son. He didn't want to get with the program, but his best friend, Ralph, genuinely got saved. Ralph is like our fourth son. He grew up in our home, and we love him as one of our own. With Ralph's newfound faith, he no longer wanted to go out with Adam at night. Instead he wanted to stay home with his best friend's mother and pray! Does God have a sense of humor or what?

This infuriated Adam. He would say things like, "I don't want your

God. Leave me alone!" I would think, "Well, that's not gonna happen." I couldn't be deterred, and I wouldn't be denied! God promised me, and that was all I needed. Then the clocks of heaven and earth came into perfect synchronization. The "appointed time" had come! My gory was about to be for His glory!

Don't Give Up!

God saved them *all*, one by one, just as He promised! He saved my middle son, Jordan, on a Sunday and my oldest son, Adam, the following Tuesday night. Chris would come a bit later. Not only did God save them, but remember the youth ministry we spent almost a decade praying for? Well, little did I know that I was raising up the youth leaders right under my nose. The week my son Adam got saved, he laid hands on his dad as he was leaving to speak at a men's conference and prayed from the Book of Ezekiel. I couldn't believe my ears, but the Holy Spirit said, "My word *never* returns void, but it *always* accomplishes what it has been set forth to do!" He said my husband and I had spoon-fed our children God's Word all of these years. It was lying dormant deep down inside of them, but once they got saved, it ignited with the Holy Spirit deep inside and became life to their dry bones!

Adam gave up his college scholarship in Rhode Island where he was doing all his dirty work. He heard the Holy Spirit say to him, "What doth it profit a man if he gains the whole world but loses his soul?" He went to a college in New York City and worked on the maintenance team in our church. While he was vacuuming his dad's office one day in August, he had a vision of a youth explosion. In the spirit he saw the building filled with teens, though at that time we didn't have nearly the number he saw in our church. The Holy Spirit directed him to have a youth rally the Friday evening after Thanksgiving.

So Adam, Jordan, and Ralph began to prepare. They would gather to pray and fast for the youth in the neighborhood. They went to war. The intercessory prayer ministry joined with them. God was now closing the generation gap. Teens were starting to get saved, and the ones who were saved before were now on fire. It's as though they came out of the woodwork. The whole paradigm shifted in the spirit. Before, if you were a Christian and wanted to serve God, you were the odd man out. But now, if you *didn't* want to serve God you were the odd one. It became very uncomfortable to live in compromise.

My middle son, Jordan, the graffiti artist, made club cards, and the youth went out to canvass the neighborhood advertising the first Youth Explosion. Many well-meaning older saints said, "Well, don't be disappointed if God doesn't fill the building. Maybe He meant that the building would be filled with His presence." My son would simply answer, "God said it will be filled with both!" Well, that night finally arrived—and there was a line around the block. Young people with their hats on backward and their pants sagging down to the floor were in line. Some were wearing their gang colors.

The meeting started, and the presence of the Lord enveloped that place. It was filled from top to bottom. Kids were even in the risers. About one thousand kids, mostly unsaved, showed up—and so did God! They ran to the altar, throwing in their knives and gang colors for a whole new set of armor. The rest is history!

I prayed for sons, and God gave me men of God! Youth Explosion has been featured in *Vibe* magazine, and on BET, BBC, and MTV. My son Adam is now our executive pastor, and our son Chris took over the youth ministry. He changed the name to Misfit! It is still growing strong. Chris has stood on the platforms of some of the largest ministries around the world. His book *Misfit* is on its seventh printing—and to think that when he was younger, he had ADHD and his kindergarten teacher told me he was stupid! Boy, would I like to have a parent-teacher conference with her today.

My middle son became a missionary in Lima, Peru, and because of his amazing accomplishments in that country, he became the regional director for Operation Blessing's work in South America, Central America, and Mexico. He has been to multiple presidential palaces and has brought some of them and their family members to Christ. When I was pregnant with him, the Holy Spirit told me to name him Jordan because he would cross over many lands. And just as God said, Jordan has done. Jordan is now home and runs our Legacy Center, which is the humanitarian arm of Christ Tabernacle. His ministry has built homes for victims of Hurricane Sandy, thanks to support from Joyce Meyer Ministries!

Legacy Center is amazing! Jordan's goal is to provide *good* food for the 55,000 homeless in New York City, 22,000 of whom are children, by purchasing food trucks. The center has a 10,000-squarefoot warehouse, which is called The Store, and each week it gives thousands of hurting families an opportunity to get brand-new, free furnishings for their apartments. They also provide thousands of backpacks for the schools in the less fortunate neighborhoods. His dream is to open up a Dream Center in New York City.

Ralph went on to earn his master's degree at New York University. He is brilliant. He is one of our teaching pastors on staff and one of the most creative and anointed orators alive. He has influenced literally thousands of youth and young adults in this generation. He has encouraged them not only to get their college degrees but to also be an influence in their high schools and universities.

Parents, don't wait until your children spin out of control to go to war. Start praying when they are little. Hannah dressed little Samuel in a linen ephod when he was a child. That means she dressed him as a priest long before he ever did anything priestly. Dress your children in words of affirmation and destiny when they are young. Hannah adjusted that ephod to size year after year. Take God's Word and adjust it to your child's understanding as he grows in the admonition of the Lord.

Little did I know that standing up and receiving the gift of faith that changed the way the brain of my heart was wired also would change my prayer life and the way all of us as intercessors prayed. It changed the course of my children's lives, our youth, and our community. Crime went down, truancy went down, graffiti went down, and graduation went up. Dances and clubs in the neighborhood had to shut down because all the kids were waiting in line to get into the Friday night youth meeting to dance before the Lord! And the public school system, which threw the name of God out, has asked our church to come in and speak to their youth. But most of all, that gift of faith changed the life and culture of our church!

Had this generation not gotten saved, we would have become extinct like dinosaurs! Now the way youth ministry is done throughout the United States has been changed. Buses from other states come just to be a part of the youth meeting. When there is a fire, everyone will be drawn to it. You don't have to advertise a fire. The fire is what draws the people. Those young people with the saggy pants are now pastors, deacons, worship leaders, and musicians in our church. They are among the most anointed and gifted of this generation!

God needs to raise up a generation of Hannahs who will *stand up* and not *give up*! A generation that will change their posture. A generation that refuses to accept lifelessness and barrenness. A generation that will not give up, but give birth!

But first, before we can stand up for others, we must stand up for ourselves. We must take our stand and receive the incredible, amazing love that God has for each and every one of us. We must allow the truth of this overwhelming, undeserved love to wash every crack and crevice deep within—cleansing everything that would dare mock, question, or try to reject that incomparable love.

Now is the time to change your position, stand up, and freely accept every blessing God has for you. You will know beyond the shadow of a doubt that you have made the eighteen-inch journey successfully when you start to immerse yourself daily in the pool of His amazing grace, naturally accepting His love instead of rejecting it. In turn, you will also be able to love others unconditionally, because you know that you know beyond the shadow of a doubt that you are unconditionally loved. The *revelation* of His love will bring about a *revolution*!

Church, we need a *revolution*! It has to start with us! It has to start in the fertile womb of a clean heart, which will be impregnated with holy Seed and thus produce spiritual children. As parents, we gave birth to them a first time, so it is up to us to give birth again!

Nehemiah said, and I paraphrase, "After I looked at the situation, I *stood up* and spoke to the people and said, 'Do not be afraid of them. Remember the Lord, great and awesome, and *fight* for your sons and daughters'" (Neh. 4:14). In Psalm 106:30 Phinehas the priest stood up and the plague was checked. Judges 5:7 says, "Village life ceased. It ceased until I, Deborah, arose [stood up]; I arose like a mother in Israel" (mev).

Don't ever *give up*—*stand up* and fight for what belongs to you.

Remember, God's kingdom suffers violence, but the violent (in the spirit) take it by force (Matt. 11:12). There's always some *gory* before He pours out His *glory*, but there is an *appointed time*.

Wait for it. Though it tarry, it will not delay!

Let's Pray

Lord, I don't have the gift of faith, but I am coming to You, the giver of this gift. I'm asking You to baptize me with the faith I need to believe that what You did for others, You will do for me. Give me the stamina to fight and wait until I see my prayers come to pass—until I see the "appointed time" come in my life. In Jesus's precious name, amen.

Maria Durso

CONCLUSION – THE HEART OF THE MATTER

Throughout this book we have seen that the heart has a mind of its own, and that many of us need to rewire the way the brain of the heart thinks. Well, everything you've read until now was to get to the nitty-gritty, the heart of why the heart must be transformed— why we must take the eighteen-inch leap to victory.

In Matthew 22:36–40 a Pharisee, an expert in the law, asked Jesus, "Which is the greatest commandment in the Law?" Jesus answered, "You shall love the Lord your God with *all your heart, and with all your soul, and with all your mind*" (mev, emphasis added). (Notice that Jesus made a distinction between the heart, soul, and mind; clearly these are the three different battlefronts that must be conquered. But note that the heart was number one.) He went on to say, "This is the first and great commandment. And the second is like it: 'You shall love your neighbor as yourself.' On these two commandments hang all the Law and the Prophets" (mev).

Jesus, who was the fulfillment of the law, summed up the whole economy of heaven in two short sentences. This is the crux of the matter. Right here we can see what's number one on God's priority list. It should cause us to take a good look deep down inside our hearts to see where the Great Physician might need to place His scalpel.

In this passage in Matthew Jesus makes no distinction between loving Him and loving our neighbor. In the answer He gives, they are one and the same. They're interchangeable! He is saying that if we love Him without reservation, we will also love others in the same manner. We could also flip it around and say if we love others with reservation, then we love God with reservation.

Jesus was basically saying that the one and only way we could show God that we love Him is by loving our neighbor. Think about it. What other way possible is there to show God our love? After all, we can't buy God flowers. He created them and is surrounded by gardens of them! We can't buy Him cologne. He is the fragrance that turns every stench into a sweet-smelling aroma!

So let's examine this basic question from the experts in the law along with Jesus's reply. First and foremost, what we must understand is that the law these experts were inquiring about and the law Jesus was referring to in His response were two totally different laws. The teachers of the law, and the One who was the fulfillment of the law, were on two different wavelengths. When Jesus was speaking about God's law, He was speaking about the law of love, which was "heaven's law" that promoted kindness and could only come from a heart that had been made whole.

On the flipside, to those experts in the law, the law was about the six hundred or so man-made rules that included various regulations, dietary restrictions, and requirements for one's outward appearance. It was a religious checklist of sorts. Even though their law meant everything to the Pharisees, their interest in the law wasn't for the betterment of others. To them it was something to get a degree in, an ego builder of sorts, a source of pride, a badge of self-righteousness that afforded them a front-row seat in the synagogue!

As we know, there was a downside to their expertise. The Bible says that knowledge puffs up, and they were as puffed up as a soufflé—high and mighty . . . that is, mighty *sad*!

Love, on the other hand, builds others up. So when the experts in the law engaged Jesus in this conversation, they were not interested in how Jesus could possibly teach them something or possibly change their hearts. *No*, they were interested in engaging Jesus in a mind game, not in having a heart-to-heart conversation. The Pharisees' game was all about who knew more than who. But the game we should be striving to master is all about who loves more than who.

The law of God, unfortunately, was nothing more to these "experts" than a subject matter to debate and discuss all day long. They used it as a weapon against those who would not be considered experts in the law.

Even though the law was their life, it never changed their lives the way God's law of love is intended to. For them, everything concerning God was north of the neck. They never gave heaven's law a chance to travel down those eighteen inches to where it would finally be able to transform them and, in turn, transform their communities.

As born-again believers we must allow God's love to travel down into the deepest recesses of our hearts so they can be melted and become like the very heart of God. When we don't allow the love of God to penetrate and permeate the hidden places of the heart and bring healing to it, we will be just like those so-called experts. We will focus on the wrong law!

When the love of God is not the supreme law that rules the mind of our hearts, we will be judgmental and prideful—nothing more than decorated religious jars, void of God's love on the inside. We will be like those who spout off religious phrases, carry signs on a picket line, and speak in "Christianese," but do little or nothing to lift the burden from those who are in pain.

The only beneficiary in our big show is us, the showoffs. The sad part is that we can easily survive and even thrive in a church environment where many of the people are as unhealthy as we are! We become people who, though "born again," strain out a gnat but swallow a camel—and miss the big picture. (See Matthew 23:24.)

Jesus, on the other hand, was just interested in getting out His Father's message of love. He just wanted to simplify all the manmade laws, cut to the chase, and reduce the complicated debacle to two simple concepts that were, in fact, really one and the same: love the Lord with every part of your heart and mind, and you will, in turn, love your neighbor as yourself. But it doesn't stop there! Your neighbor, the beneficiary of this kind of love, will then be melted by the divine, supernatural love of God that pours out of you and will one day pour it out onto someone else. When our hearts are whole, it creates a domino effect!

Now here is the problem, the crux of the matter. It is impossible to love your neighbor as much as you love yourself if you don't love God with your *whole heart*. And it is impossible to love God with your *whole heart* unless your *heart* is whole!

Do you now see why having a healthy heart is of the utmost importance? Do you see why knowing God's Word in your mind isn't enough? Do you now see that the heart must be whole in order for us to love God and in turn love our neighbor? This was all that mattered to Jesus, who was God in the flesh. When we love God with a whole heart, the by-product, of course, is that we will not only truly love our neighbor, but we will also look for ways to be kind to one another and thus allow heaven to come down to earth.

In Luke 10 another so-called expert in the law asked Jesus, "Who is my neighbor?" (v. 29). And Jesus pointed out that the real hero in that story was the good Samaritan. A Samaritan—not the priest or the Levite, those who had respectable titles. No, they crossed the street when they saw the unnamed bleeding man. They were too busy getting to and from their religious duties to stop and help the man.

They were kind of like us. We are so involved in our committees, our Bible studies, and our choir practices that we often have no time for the people who are bleeding on the roadside. Too often we are either hurrying to get home from church or rushing to be on time for service.

I don't think the priest or the Levite intentionally thought, "I'll just leave that guy bleeding there. It's not my problem." No, I just think that because their *hearts weren't whole*, they couldn't see what was really important to God. They were focused on crossing every t and dotting every i because they thought, in the twisted thinking of their heart, that this was what God was interested in!

A New Level

Another major problem created when the heart is not whole is that we can't love ourselves, which we must do if we are to love one another. When we hate ourselves, we hate the world. When we are angry and dissatisfied with ourselves, we are angry and dissatisfied with everything and everyone around us.

But the New Testament gives us another challenge. It tells us to not only love our neighbor as we love ourselves, but to also love our neighbor as Christ has loved us! Whoa, that's a pretty tall order, but we don't have to do this alone! We have living on the inside of us the Helper, the Holy Spirit, who empowers us to go to a new level—a new level of maturity, a new level of courage. To be able to love others as He has loved us takes real maturity. And that's the apex of our faith. Yes, that's the "new level" we should be striving for—not the "new level" of deeper revelation so we can put all our knowledge on display, thus walking around wearing a smug grin that says, "I know more than you." *So not mature!*

God's Word challenges us in Hebrews 3:13–15 to encourage one another daily, as long as it's called "today," lest the devil bring discouragement to our brothers or sisters, causing them to *lose heart*. Mature believers are always looking to encourage others, because their hearts are overflowing with God's love. In order to be an encourager, you need to be looking away from yourself to the betterment of others. People in the body of Christ who are encouragers are single-handedly responsible for snatching many a saint from the hand of the enemy, because they had the courage to step in and lift them up with an anointed word from heaven!

Did you know that in psychology there is something called "withholding"? The person whose heart is not whole will purposely withhold encouragement from someone else for fear that the encouraging word will put them on their same level. This goes on in the body of Christ all the time. We withhold compliments and godly honor because we fear someone else will rise up and be greater than we are. Jesus made Himself nothing, of no reputation, so He could make us great. Oh, may the Holy Spirit make us whole—heart-healthy and practicing the gift of encouragement daily.

What good is it if I know who the Antichrist is if I don't love? If I have not love, according to God's economy I am nothing (1 Cor. 13:1–3)—a big, fat zero (and I don't mean a size zero!). *What good is it if we speak in tongues but don't speak in kind?*

First Peter 4:8 sums it all up: *"Most importantly, love each other deeply"* (ncv, emphasis added), because love has a way of *not* looking at others' sins. People who are experts in the law but not experts on God's love use the law to point out others' flaws, yet God sent Jesus to fulfill the law so that He could overlook our flaws and extend love. The law that is man-made looks *at* others' faults, whereas God's law of love looks *away* from others' weaknesses.

In the way God loves, He can definitely be accused of being involved in many a "cover-up." I want to do that too! I want to be in the "covering" business instead of the "exposing" business. I want to give mercy out the same way God poured His mercy in, but if my heart is not made whole, I will be blind to all the mercy that has been afforded me.

The Bible says in Romans 13:8, "Let no debt remain outstanding, except the continuing debt to love one another." Because we can't pay God back for all He has done for us, we must pay it forward. How will we ever get to pay that outstanding debt to love one another if we can't get past the issues about ourselves that we have "stored up" in our heart's brain? How can we ever pay it forward if our hearts are not thinking heaven's thoughts?

I pray that the Holy Spirit will use this book to get to the real "heart" of the matter: the matters of the heart! The heart seals the deal. As a man thinks *in his heart*—that is who he really is!

Please, take the eighteen-inch challenge with me, and allow the Holy Spirit to uproot the thorns that have been sown and cultivated in the ground of our hearts. We have eaten their bitter fruit far too long. Let's allow the Lord to replant seeds of His magnanimous love in our hearts so the world can taste and see that He is good!

Let's Pray

Lord, please clean my heart thoroughly. Take Your scalpel and gut out all the infection that keeps my heart sick once and for all. Make me totally whole so I can finally fulfill the purpose I was created for. Allow me to be a force to be reckoned with as I spread Your love and encouragement wherever You place me, so the world will know the Savior who truly loves them unconditionally! In Jesus's name, amen.

NOTES

Introduction

1. As quoted in Mark C. Crowley, *Lead From the Heart: Transformational Leadership for the 21st Century* (Bloomington, IN: Balboa Press, 2011), 41.
2. Dr. Caroline Leaf, "The Three Brains," http://drleaf.com/about/ scientific-philosophy/ (accessed October 7, 2014).

Chapter 2 – We Need A Brain Wash

1. Richard Shears, "Do Hearts Have Memories? Transplant Patient Gets Craving for Food Eaten by Organ Donor," Mail Online, December 23, 2009, http://www.dailymail.co.uk/news/article-1237998/Heart-transplant-patient-gets-craving-food-eaten-organ-donor.html (accessed October 15, 2014).
2. *World Book Encyclopedia*, vol. 8 (Chicago, IL: World Book Inc., 1989), s.v "grasshoppers."
3. Ibid.

Chapter 5 – Does *Favor* Mean *Favorite*?

1. Frances J. Roberts, Come Away My Beloved (Uhrichsville, OH: Barbour Publishing, Inc., 2002), "Rain."

Chapter 7 – Heart Attacks

2. As told by Ed Gungor in *Religiously Transmitted Diseases* (Nashville, TN: Thomas Nelson, 2006), 214. See also Lawrence O. Richards, *The Expository Dictionary of Bible Words* (Grand Rapids, MI: Zondervan, 1984) and *Spirit-Filled Life Bible NKJV* (Nashville, TN: Thomas Nelson, 1991), footnote on 1549.

Chapter 8 – Complexes . . . Will They Ever Go Away?

1. YouTube.com, "Lady Gaga Presents: Gaga Revealed," https://www.youtube.com/watch?v=M0bNHxHeTZQ (accessed October 29, 2014).
2. Brian Hiatt, "Deep Inside the Unreal World of Lady Gaga," *Rolling Stone*, June 9, 2011, http://www.rollingstone.com/music/news/deep-inside -the-unreal-world-of-lady-gaga-20110609 (accessed October 29, 2014).
3. Katie Kindelan, "Kevin Costner Surprised by Link to Whitney Houston," ABC News, May 24, 2012, accessed October 24, 2014, http:// abcnews.go.com/blogs/entertainment/2012/05/kevin-costner-surprised-by -link-to-whitney-houston/.
4. Rick Renner, *Sparkling Gems From the Greek* (Tulsa, OK: Teach All Nations, 2003), 856.
5. Ibid., 852–853.
6. Peter J. Blackburn, "Dwight L Moody," Heroes of the Faith, 1999, http://peterjblackburn.net/people/moody.htm (accessed October 15, 2014).
7. Elizabeth Ruth Skoglund, *Bright Days, Dark Nights: With Charles Spurgeon in Triumph Over Emotional Pain* (Grand Rapids, MI: Baker Books, 2000).
8. C.H. Spurgeon, *Chequebook of the Bank of Faith: Daily Readings* (n.p.: Christian Focus Publications, 2005), 215; see also "August 2, Speak What He Teaches," accessed October 7, 2014, http://www.spurgeon.org/fcb/ fcb-bod.htm.

Chapter 9 — There Is Treasure In The Trash

1. *World Book Encyclopedia*, vol. 8, s.v. "sheep.".
2. Mike Bullivant, "Lanolin, Wool and Hand Cream," PBS.org, http://www.pbs.org/weta/roughscience/series3/shakers/handcream.html (accessed November 6, 2014).
3. Microsoft Encarta Online Encyclopedia 2006, s.v. "lanolin." No longer available online. See also Lanolin.com, "From Fleece to Grease," http://www.lanolin.com/lanolin-basics/from-fleece-to-grease.html (accessed November 6, 2014).
4. Lawrence O. Richards, *Expository Dictionary of Bible Words* (Grand Rapids, MI: Zondervan, 1991).
5. As quoted in L. B. Cowman, *Streams in the Desert* (Grand Rapids, MI: Zondervan, 1997), "August 13," 309.
6. Rick Warren, Facebook post, June 25, 2011, accessed September 12, 2014, https://www.facebook.com/pastorrickwarren/posts/10150303272390903?comment_id=18534102.
7. Andrew Alexander Bonar, *Andrew A. Bonar, D.D., Diary and Letters* (London: Hodder and Stoughton, 1894), 192.

Chapter 10 — All Access

1. *Strong's Greek Lexicon*, G4318, s.v. "*prosagōgē*," Blue Letter Bible, http://www.blueletterbible.org/lang/Lexicon/Lexicon.cfm?Strongs=G4318&t=KJV (accessed October 7, 2014).
2. *Strong's Greek Lexicon*, G3954, s.v. "*parrēsia*," Blue Letter Bible, http://www.blueletterbible.org/lang/Lexicon/Lexicon.cfm?Strongs=G3954&t=KJV (accessed October 7, 2014).

ABOUT THE AUTHOR

aria Durso is living proof that if anyone is in Christ, he is a new creation (2 Corinthians 5:17). Having come from a childhood devastated by loss and abuse she grew up to thinking she could mask her pain with drugs. Her lifestyle could have left her hopeless and alone—yet God kept and preserved Maria's life.

Understanding firsthand the effects of abandonment, loneliness and rejection are, she ministers to those whose hurt lies deep in the heart and works to minister to those who need hope. Armed with discernment, insight into the true character of God, honest about her own experience, and down to earth, Maria is an intercessor, teacher, and powerful speaker.

In 1975, immediately following the first most important walk Maria would ever take down a church aisle—Maria took her second most important walk down the aisle and married her life-long love, Michael Durso. Together she has pastored along side of her husband, Senior Pastor Michael Durso at Christ Tabernacle, the first church to be birthed from The Brooklyn Tabernacle, since 1985. They have witnessed, firsthand, the faithfulness and grace of God who supplies the needs of a continually growing urban church.

Believing that our greatest ministry is prayer, she oversees the Prayer Band, a group that intercedes daily for the needs of the congregation, various ministries, the Pastoral staff and requests that are phoned in to the church. Maria also oversees the Women's Ministry at Christ Tabernacle, a ministry that encourages women through fellowship, worship, and the Word of God.

Maria recently published her first book, *From Your Head to Your Heart*. With powerful examples from the Bible and redeeming stories from her testimony involving abandonment, loneliness, rejection, and drug use—this book will give you the keys to access the power in God's Word. Begin the renewing journey from your head to your heart today.

Blessed with a wonderful husband and three sons in ministry, their wives and grandmother to eight, Maria considers herself wholly blessed. The Durso's look forward to the great plans God has for their ministry, their lives, and their family.

God continues to open doors for her to minister in conferences, seminars, and retreats. Connect with Maria Durso at MariaDurso.com.